Test Your Prepositions

Pearson Education Limited
Edinburgh Gate
Harlow
Essex CM20 2JE, England
and Associated Companies throughout the world.

ISBN 0 582 45172 8

First published 1990
This edition published 2001
Text copyright © Peter Watcyn-Jones and Jake Allsop 1990, 2001

Designed and typeset by Pantek Arts Ltd, Maidstone, Kent
Test Your format devised by Peter Watcyn-Jones
Illustrations by Peter Standley
Printed in Italy by Rotolito Lombarda

Published by Pearson Education Limited in association with Penguin Books Ltd, both companies being subsidiaries of Pearson plc.

For a complete list of the titles available from Penguin English please visit our website at www.penguinenglish.com, or write to your local Pearson Education office or to: Marketing Department, Penguin Longman Publishing, 80 Strand, London WC2R 0RL.

Contents

Section 1: Prepositions of time and place

This section looks at the use of prepositions to show the relationship between people, things and events.

Prepositions can express relationships in TIME, answering the question 'When?', e.g. *Let's meet **on** Friday, **at** three o'clock and chat **for** a while.*

They can express relationships in SPACE, answering the question 'Where?', e.g. *He lived alone **in** an old house **on** the edge of the village.*

They can also express many other kinds of relationships such as PURPOSE, e.g. *You ought to have a dog **for** company*, POSSESSION, e.g. *The other side **of** the garden*, and RESULT, e.g. *A verdict of death **from** drowning.*

'You'll have to make your own bed from now on.'

1 Describing a room

Look at the drawing and fill in the missing prepositions and prepositional phrases in the sentences below. Choose from the following but only use each word or phrase once.

above	behind	below	between	in	in front of	next to	on
	~~opposite~~	to the left of		to the right of		under	

1   The sofa is ___*opposite*___ the armchair.

2   The clock is _____ the mantelpiece.

3   The mobile phone is _____ the table.

4   The painting is _____ the fireplace.

5   The bookcase is _____ the fireplace.

6   The glasses are _____ the bottle.

7   The flowers are _____ the vase.

8   The coffee table is _____ the sofa and the armchair.

9   The cat is _____ the armchair.

10   The CD-player is _____ the TV.

11   The clock is _____ the painting.

12   The book is _____ the vase of flowers.

 Prepositions can be simple, consisting of a single word, e.g. *in*, or compound, consisting of more than one word, e.g. *in front of*.

2 Following directions

Jane has written to her friend Lucy, giving her instructions on how to reach her house. Look at the map and fill in the missing prepositions in the letter.

Dear Lucy,

Thanks for your letter. It's quite easy to find my house. When you get
(1) __**off**__ the bus, start walking (2) _____ the High Street
(3) _____ the church. (4) _____ the way, you'll pass a pub called
The King's Head and a telephone box. Just (5) _____ the telephone box,
(6) _____ the left, is a car park. Go (7) _____ the car park and
continue (8) _____ the footpath that goes (9) _____ Box Wood.
Turn right (10) _____ the signpost and walk (11) _____ the river
bank until you come (12) _____ a bridge. Don't go (13) _____ the
bridge but keep on walking until you reach a cottage called Hillside.
(14) _____ the cottage is a narrow road that leads (15) _____
a farm. Follow the road and turn left just before you reach the farm.
(16) _____ the end of this road is a row of houses. I live (17) _____
the middle house. It's number 10 and has a lamppost (18) _____ it.
If I'm not in, go (19) _____ the back where you'll find a spare key to the
front door (20) _____ the right (21) _____ the back door,
(22) _____ a flowerpot. I hope you don't get lost!

I'm looking forward to seeing you again.

Lots of love,

Jane

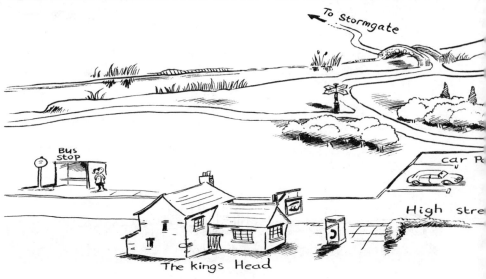

At or in?

At describes where you are in a general way without defining whether you are *in*, *under*, *behind*, etc., e.g. *I'm sitting **at** my desk*.

In (like *under*, *behind*, etc.) can be more specific, e.g. *I keep my pens **in** my desk*.

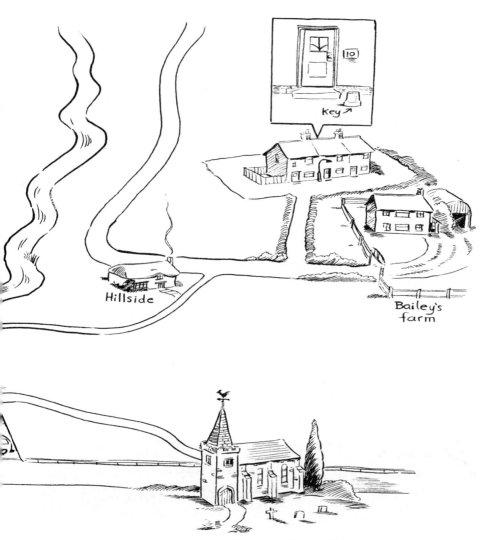

5 Pairs of prepositions

The following pairs of phrases or sentences are very similar. Choose a suitable preposition for each pair.

| 1 | above/over | She put a blanket __over__ her knees to keep warm. |
| | | She was wearing a skirt that came just _above_ the knee. |

| 2 | at/in | We arrived _____ Zurich. |
| | | We arrived _____ Zurich airport. |

| 3 | on/on to | The cat loved to sleep _____ the sofa. |
| | | The cat jumped off the table and _____ the sofa. |

| 4 | below/under | A lot of Holland is _____ sea level. |
| | | Atlantis was a city _____ the sea. |

| 5 | in/into | The police burst _____ the room and arrested everyone. |
| | | The police were already _____ the room when I arrived. |

| 6 | at/to | I have to go _____ the doctor's for a check-up. |
| | | She is _____ the doctor's, having a check-up. |

| 7 | before/ in front of | I was _____ you in the queue. |
| | | Whose is that van _____ the house? |

| 8 | in/on | I'm leaving _____ Tuesday morning. |
| | | See you _____ the morning. |

| 9 | at/in | Things that go 'bump' _____ the night! |
| | | The sky _____ night |

| 10 | At/In | _____ five o'clock exactly |
| | | _____ five minutes' time |

| 11 | for/since | We've been waiting _____ three o'clock. |
| | | We've been waiting _____ three hours. |

| 12 | among/ between | In this photo I'm standing _____ my two best friends. |
| | | It's great to be _____ friends. |

13   out of/outside   The dog jumped _____ the box and into the dustbin.

The dog was _____ the door, whining to be let in.

14   above/over   'Hey diddle diddle, the cat and the fiddle, the cow jumped _____ the moon.' (children's nursery rhyme)

That cow is definitely _____ average!

15   by/until   Wait _____ sunset and then leave.

Leave _____ sunset at the latest.

16   by/within   The bill must be paid _____ 30 days.

The bill must be paid _____ the end of the month.

17   during/ through   She slept _____ the whole thing!

Don't talk _____ the concert.

18   near/next to   Come and sit _____ me.

Is your house far from town? No, it's quite _____ the centre.

19   by/on   'I met my true love down _____ the riverside.' (song)

There are lots of people boating _____ the river.

20   below/under   If you are _____ eighteen, they won't let you see that film.

Once the exchange rate falls _____ a certain level, the bank will take action.

We say *since* a point of time, but *for* a period of time.

To suggests movement; *at* suggests a point you have reached in space or time.

Above/below suggest higher/lower than.

By means not later than a point in time; *within* means not later than a period of time.

6 Joke time 1

Complete the following jokes by filling in the missing prepositions. All the completed phrases are expressions of time or place.

1 Teacher: Where are you ___*from*___ ?
   Student: Germany.
   Teacher: Which part?
   Student: All of me.

2 An old lady went _____ the optician's and said: 'I need a new pair of glasses.'
   The optician replied: 'I knew that as soon as you walked _____ the window.'

3 Doctor: Good morning, Mrs Gibbs. I haven't seen you _____ a long time.
   Mrs Gibbs: I know, doctor. I've been ill.

4 Question: What's the fastest vegetable _____ the world?
   Answer: A runner bean.

5 Teacher: If we breathe oxygen _____ the daytime, what do we breathe _____ night?
   Student: Nitrogen?

6 Patient: Doctor! Doctor! I think I'm a dog.
   Doctor: Sit down, please.
   Patient: I can't. I'm not allowed _____ the furniture.

7 Doctor: Did you drink your orange juice after your bath?
   Patient: _____ drinking the bath I didn't have much room for the orange juice.

8 Man: I had to give up tap dancing.
   Woman: Why?
   Man: I kept falling _____ the sink.

9 Man: What's the best way to remove paint _____ a chair?
   Shopkeeper: Sit down _____ it before it's dry.

10 Man: My neighbours bang _____ the wall _____ all hours.
    Friend: Doesn't that keep you awake?
    Man: No, but _____ a while I just can't go on with my trumpet practice!

11 James: I throw myself _____ everything I do.
    Susan: Go and dig a large hole!

Section 2:
Verb + preposition

The pattern VERB + PREPOSITION (always followed by an object), e.g. *think about*, *believe in*, is very common in English.

The meaning of the phrase may be literal, e.g. *I **looked into** the room to see who was there*, or it may be non-literal, e.g. *The police **are looking into** the disappearance of a nine-year-old boy*. In the second example, *look into* means *investigate*.

Usually the choice of preposition is obvious, but in verb phrases like *look after* (meaning *take care of*), it may not be. Some verbs are followed by a preposition which you might not expect, e.g. *depend **on*** (where you might expect ***from***).

Note that *to*, in addition to being a marker of the infinitive, e.g. *I like **to** sunbathe when I'm on holiday*, can also be a simple preposition e.g. *I look forward **to** seeing you* or *I am not used **to** getting up early*. The way to check this is to see if you can put *it* after the *to*:

*I am not used **to** getting up early.*
*I am not used **to** it.*

But:
*I like **to** sunbathe when I'm on holiday.*
~~*I like to it*~~ is not possible, so *to* here is not a preposition.

Everyone is raving about the new play at the Globe Theatre.

7 Matching pairs 1

Match each verb + preposition on the left with an object on the right.

1	enrol on ...	**a**	... miracles
2	believe in ...	**b**	... an oncoming vehicle
3	translate into ...	**c**	... an April Fool trick
4	fall behind with ...	**d**	... your knowledge of statistics
5	brush up on ...	**e**	... a course at the English Institute
6	come into ...	**f**	... the chance to interview the President
7	book into ...	**g**	... a heavy shower of rain
8	inoculate against ...	**h**	... the best hotel in town
9	jump at ...	**i**	... typhoid, cholera and yellow fever
10	fall for ...	**j**	... your credit card payments
11	shelter from ...	**k**	... a fortune
12	collide with ...	**l**	... several foreign languages

Write your answers here:

1	2	3	4	5	6	7	8	9	10	11	12
e											

8 Complete the sentences 1

Complete the sentences below with one of the following verbs plus a preposition. Remember to use the correct form of the verb.

apologize   arrive   belong   complain   correspond   die   distinguish
experiment   fill   ~~hear~~   knock   lose   pray   rhyme   suffer   vote

1   Did you _hear about_ Tom and Sally? They've decided to emigrate to New Zealand.

2   It was almost midnight when we _____ the station.

3   Do you know who this book _____ ?

4   I _____ taking so long to reply to your letter.

5   Could you _____ this form, please?

6   If you don't agree with the proposal, you can always _____ it at the meeting.

7   Some people find it difficult to _____ an American accent and a Canadian accent.

8   He _____ the manager about the poor service at the restaurant.

9   Would you say that the British House of Lords _____ the American Senate?

10   I think there's someone _____ the door.

11   Can you think of a word that _____ 'sing'? Yes, 'bring'.

12   Do you think scientists should be allowed to _____ animals?

13   The priest said he would _____ us.

14   For years, her husband had _____ migraines.

15   I don't know why, but I really hate _____ cards. It puts me in a bad mood all day.

16   Although he had survived the battle, the soldier later _____ his wounds.

The same verb can be followed by different prepositions depending on the meaning. For example, *to correspond with* someone means *to write to them*. *To correspond to* means *to be equivalent to*, e.g. *32 degrees Fahrenheit corresponds to 0 degrees Celsius*.

9 Verb groups

Place each of the following verbs under a suitable preposition (five under each). When you have finished, see if you can make sentences using each verb plus preposition.

abstain	appeal	apply	approve	believe
benefit	cater	coincide	collaborate	compensate
concentrate	consist	cope	decrease	dedicate
delight	depart	depend	dispose	dream
enrol	expel	flee	~~glance~~	hint
indulge	invest	long	marvel	object
point	quarrel	rely	respond	subscribe
sympathize	take advantage	tread	vote	wink

AT

glance
_____
_____
_____
_____

FOR

_____
_____
_____
_____
_____

FROM

_____
_____
_____
_____
_____

IN

_____
_____
_____
_____
_____

OF

_____
_____
_____
_____
_____

ON

_____
_____
_____
_____
_____

TO

_____
_____
_____
_____

WITH

_____
_____
_____
_____

 Think of the meaning of the verb. In most (but not all) cases, the choice of preposition is logical. For example, if you want a job, your PURPOSE in *applying* is to get the job. The preposition *for* often expresses purpose, so the verb phrase is *to apply for* (a job).

10 Complete the sentences 2

Complete the sentences below with one of the following verbs plus a preposition. Remember to use the correct form of the verb.

> account   accuse   book   count   deal   grumble
> insist   refrain   surround   specialize   taste   ~~translate~~

1 The Hotel's fire regulations have been _**translated into**_ eighteen languages.

2 As it was getting late, we decided to _____ the nearest hotel.

3 'My coffee _____ garlic!'
'You're lucky, mine has no taste at all.'

4 I was _____ cheating in the examination, just because I had made a few notes on the back of my hand.

5 If there are any personnel problems in the factory, the boss always asks her deputy to _____ them.

6 The English _____ the weather, but secretly they don't mind their climate because they love complaining.

7 'Why am I _____ idiots?'
'We don't know, Dad.'

8 The teacher _____ calling me 'Ghengis', even though my real name is 'Attila'.

9 Michael trained as a psychiatrist, and he now _____ mental disorders of the very rich.

10 Sylvia is always ready to help people: you can _____ her to help out in a crisis.

11 Scientists are unable to _____ the hole in the ozone layer, although some people believe that aerosols are to blame.

12 'Passengers are kindly requested to _____ smoking.' (airline announcement)

Some verbs have two objects, e.g. *grumble* **to** *the grocer* **about** *the price of butter*. Here the direct object is *butter*; the indirect object is *the grocer*. After some verbs, the indirect object does not require a preposition, e.g. *I told the waiter about the fly in my yoghurt*, compared to *I complained* **to** *the waiter about the fly in my yoghurt*.

11 Sentence transformation 1

Rewrite the following sentences using the verb in capital letters with a suitable preposition to replace the underlined words. Make each new sentence as similar in meaning as possible to the original. You may need to change the tense or the form of the verb. Choose from the following prepositions.

~~about~~	across	against	at	by	for	in	into	on	over
	round	through	to	towards	with	after			

1   Everyone is <u>full of praise</u> for the new play at the
    Globe Theatre.
    Everyone is *raving about* the new play at the   RAVE
    Globe Theatre.

2   Who's <u>taking care of</u> the children?
    Who's _____ the children?   LOOK

3   Some people <u>are opposed to</u> women with small
    children going out to work.
    Some people don't _____ women   AGREE
    with small children going out to work.

4   My dog really <u>likes you</u>.
    My dog has really_____ you.   TAKE

5   Would you like to <u>explain in more detail</u> what
    you proposed when we last spoke?
    Would you like to _____ what you   ELABORATE
    proposed when we last spoke?

6   Rachael <u>did not hesitate to take advantage of</u> the
    chance to go to Australia.
    Rachael _____ the chance to go to Australia.   JUMP

7   Will <u>I be at a disadvantage because of</u> my age?
    Will my age _____ me?   COUNT

8   Little children know how to <u>behave in such a way that</u>
their parents <u>will give them what they want</u>.
Little children know how to _____   GET
their parents.

9   The repairs we had to do on the car have
<u>really used up a lot of</u> our savings.
The repairs have _____ our savings.   EAT

10   <u>Tedious as it was</u>, I had to <u>examine</u> a large number
of documents before I found what I was looking for.
I had to _____ a large number of   PLOUGH
documents before I found what I was looking for.

11   She <u>happened to find</u> the missing necklace
while she was looking for something else.
She _____ the missing necklace   STUMBLE
while she was looking for something else.

12   Any money I have to spare is <u>added to the money</u>
<u>I am saving for</u> my holiday.
Any money I have to spare is _____   PUT
my holiday.

13   Everybody deserted John after he was arrested, but
his wife told him: 'I will <u>not abandon</u> you, John,
whatever happens.'
His wife promised to _____ him.   STICK

14   She decided to <u>treat herself to</u> a large box of
chocolates.
She decided to _____ chocolates.   INDULGE

15   During the interview, the Prime Minister tried to
<u>avoid going into detail about</u> an embarrassing story.
She tried to _____ an embarrassing story.   GLOSS

16   I am happy to <u>confirm that he is a man of</u> integrity.
I can _____ him.   VOUCH

12 Against, at, by, for, in, over

Complete the following sentences using *against, at, by, for, in* or *over*.

1 I tripped __*over*__ the cat and fell downstairs.

2 Is it true that Peter is currently involved _____ writing a book about Swedish humour?

3 The best reason for having strict rules at school is that it gives the pupils something to rebel _____ when they are older.

4 The match resulted _____ a goalless draw after extra time.

5 Most people think the government is to blame _____ rising unemployment.

6 Although I practise quite a lot, I never seem to win very often _____ tennis.

7 Think of a number. Now multiply it _____ seven.

8 I don't know his exact age. I can only guess _____ how old he really is.

9 Is it possible to insure yourself _____ nuclear attack?

10 I've been going _____ your essay and I wore out three red pens making corrections!

11 Before going to Africa, Graham had himself inoculated _____ tetanus, yellow fever, cholera and typhoid.

12 Raise the dart to eye level, aim _____ the dartboard and try to hit the bull's eye.

13 I'm longing _____ the summer holidays to arrive, aren't you?

14 What do you get if you divide 947 _____ 17?
A complicated number.

Remember that the verb following a preposition must be in the *-ing* (gerund) form, e.g. *Please refrain from **making** loud noises* (NOT ~~refrain from to make~~).

13 About, from, into, on, to

Complete the following sentences using *about*, *from*, *into*, *on* or *to*.

1. She intended to post my letter, but she forgot all __*about*__ it.

2. The film *The Magnificent Seven* was based _____ a Japanese story about the samurai.

3. Don't kiss the Prince or he might change _____ a frog.

4. How does a frog differ _____ a toad?

5. Today I feel really miserable because I can't find anything to complain _____ .

6. John was about to take his wife out to dinner when it occurred _____ him that he was not married.

7. There's a man over there with binoculars. Do you think he's a birdwatcher, or is he spying _____ us?

8. If I have problems with my homework, I know I can always call _____ my older sister to help me.

9. Resulting _____ their exhaustive research into the matter, scientists can now confirm that we are all getting older.

10. Do you pride yourself _____ looking smart, or are you simply trying to impress me?

11. Make yourself a drink while I go and change _____ something more comfortable.

12. When Tom told me _____ his quarrel with Jerry, I asked him not to involve me in his personal affairs.

13. What it amounts _____ is this: the word 'socialist' means what the government wants it to mean.

Remember: some verbs take different prepositions depending on the meaning. For example, you *call on* somebody to do something (give an invitation), and you *call for* something to be done (make a demand).

14 Sentence transformation 2

For each of the sentences below, use the verb in capital letters and a suitable preposition to write a new sentence. The new sentence should be as similar as possible in meaning to the original. You may need to change the tense or form of the verb.

1 We laughed very loudly when we saw the clown.   **ROAR**
We ___*roared with*___ laughter when we saw the clown.

2 Do you want a drink?   **CARE**
Would you _____ a drink?

3 What do the letters EU mean?   **STAND**
What do the letters EU _____ ?

4 We ran into a barn to get out of the rain.   **SHELTER**
We _____ the rain in a barn.

5 I lent my cousin £5.   **BORROW**
My cousin _____ £5 _____ me.

6 The group leader asked students if they would volunteer to help with the campaign to help earthquake victims.   **CALL**
The group leader _____ volunteers to help with the campaign.

7 A car crashed into a bus this morning.   **COLLIDE**
A car _____ a bus this morning.

8 Charlie has just inherited a fortune!   **COME**
Charlie has just _____ a fortune!

9   I have the same first name as my grandmother.   NAME
     I was _____ my grandmother.

10   Farmers' dogs will often attack people they don't   GO
     recognize.
     Farmers' dogs often _____ people
     they don't recognize.

11   I like the idea of a universal language.   APPEAL
     The idea of a universal language _____ me.

12   I was really deceived by his story about seeing an   FELL
     ostrich in his back garden!
     I really _____ his story!

13   There is a fence round the pond to stop children   PREVENT
     falling in.
     The fence is to _____ children _____ falling
     in the pond.

14   I'm not sure what you are trying to say.   DRIVE
     What are you _____ ?

15 Adverb + preposition pairs

Complete each of the sentences using one of these adverb + preposition pairs.

around for	around to	away for	away with	back on
behind with	down to	down with	in for	in with	on at
~~out for~~	over to	up on	up to	up with

---

1   If you go into the park alone at night, watch _____ *out for* _____ pickpockets.

---

2   If you can't do the job, why don't you hand it _____ someone else?

---

3   I've had so many other things to do lately that I've fallen _____ my studies. Never mind, I'll soon catch up.

---

4   I've been looking _____ somewhere to live, but I haven't found anything suitable yet.

---

5   When the sky is red in the morning, it means we are _____ some bad weather.

---

6   Is Pat ill again? He's forever going _____ some illness or other!

---

7   Just because I kissed you last night, don't run _____ the idea that I am serious about you.

---

8   'When are you going to mend that broken window?'
'Don't worry, I'll get _____ it one of these days.'

---

9   I didn't bring any money with me. If you pay for the meal, I'll settle _____ you later.

10   If you're going to apply for that interpreter's job, you'd better brush _____ your French and German.

11   'When shall we meet for lunch?'
'Well, I'm free any time, so I'll fit _____ your plans.'

12   He thinks he's superior to everyone else. That's why he always talks _____ people.

13   My sister was very disappointed when she went to see the Backstreet Boys in concert. She said the group failed to live _____ her expectations!

14   My parents nag me constantly. They keep _____ me to smarten myself up and get a proper job.

15   When money is short, you have to think about cutting _____ luxuries.

16   'Did you get this booklet from a bookshop?'
'No, I had to write _____ it.'

Think of these three-part verb phrases as a verb with two parts (verb + adverb) followed by a preposition. For example, think of *keep on at* as *keep on + at*, rather than as *keep + on at*.

16 Verb + preposition crossword

Read through the sentences below and complete the crossword. The missing words are either verbs (in various tenses) or prepositions.

Across

2   David's a bit odd, isn't he? He actually _____ rain to sunshine (7).

5   A '___ away' is a place where you go so that nobody will find you (4).

7   We _____ to France on the ferrry (9).

10   Stop _____ at me! I'm not deaf, you know (8).

11   She shared her birthday cake _____ her friends (5).

13   I don't like being in a crowded theatre, so I always try to sit _____ an exit (4).

15   The driver lost control of his car and crashed _____ a lamppost (4).

17   We tried to get everyone to _____ in the dancing (4).

18   Both the candidates were so well qualified that it was very difficult to choose _____ them (7).

20   If you don't agree with the verdict of the court you can always appeal _____ it (7).

21   The next train for Stansted airport will depart _____ platform 6 (4).

24   'What do you get if you _____ 14 by 12?' '168.' (8)

26   Yoshiko loves Shakespeare; she's always quoting passages _____ his plays (4).

27   Let me just make a _____ of your e-mail address and I'll send you an e-mail as soon as I get home (4).

28   My job is very international. I work _____ people from all over the world (4).

Down

1   We went under the bridge to _____ from the rain (7).

3   One of Andrew Lloyd-Webber's most famous songs is 'Don't cry _____ me, Argentina' (3).

4   If it's too small you can always go back to the shop and _____ it for a larger one (8).

6   I have a poor memory so I have to write everything _____ in this little book (4).

8   MusakTV is a really bad channel: everybody complains _____ the rubbish they show (5).

9   Very few prisoners ever managed to _____ from Devil's Island (6).

12   Milk will soon _____ off in hot weather (2).

14   After a long dry spell, everybody _____ for a really heavy shower of rain (5).

15 Has Michael _____ you to his party on Saturday? (7)

16 You remind me _____ my father: he had big ears just like yours! (2)

19 You needn't _____ about Liz. She'll be all right. She knows how to look after herself (5).

22 Don't try to _____ me for the accident! I wasn't even here when it happened (5).

23 He was very shy and didn't like _____ with people, especially strangers (6).

25 Would you like one of these cakes? They're _____ over from yesterday's birthday party (4).

26 Does the River Thames _____ into the North Sea or the English Channel? (4)

29 The judge sentenced him _____ six months' imprisonment (2).

Section 3:
Noun + preposition

This section looks at the patterns NOUN + PREPOSITION, e.g. *a cure for, the opposite of,* and VERB + NOUN + PREPOSITION, e.g. *pay a visit to, take advantage of.*

There are also many expressions (sometimes called compound prepositions) with the pattern PREPOSITION + NOUN + PREPOSITION, e.g. *on account of, by virtue of, for the sake of, in addition to, in favour of.* Learn these compound prepositions as whole phrases.

Often the choice of preposition depends on the meaning of a noun, e.g. *an interest in, a demand for, in addition to.* Sometimes the preposition is unexpected, e.g. *an aversion **to**,* where you might expect ***from**.*

'Do you know of a cure for hiccups?'

17 Matching pairs 2

Match the phrases in the two columns. Note which preposition is used with each noun.

1	She is undergoing treatment ...	a	... in wildlife.
2	A bright student with an aptitude ...	b	... of the theatre manager.
3	Congratulations ...	c	... into the causes of ageing.
4	Scientists conduct research ...	d	... for spaghetti carbonara.
5	He has fallen in love ...	e	... for learning foreign languages.
6	The Princess is heir ...	f	... on your arms and shoulders.
7	Coffee drinkers have a choice ...	g	... for a serious illness.
8	Free tickets with the compliments ...	h	... between black and white.
9	Kenya is a country rich ...	i	... to the Dutch throne.
10	It is time for the children to pay a visit ...	j	... with the girl next door.
11	The Italian chef gave me a recipe ...	k	... on your Wedding Anniversary!
12	Working constantly at a computer puts a strain ...	l	... to their grandparents.

Write your answers here:

1	2	3	4	5	6	7	8	9	10	11	12
g											

18 Fill the gaps 1

Complete the sentences below with one of the following nouns plus a preposition.

basis	campaign	choice	control	cruelty	excuse	fall	freedom
genius	anger	knowledge	objection	~~opposite~~	strain	problem	

1 What is the __*opposite of*__ 'timid'? Is it 'bold' or 'brave'?

2 The _____ chewing gum is that it loses its flavour too quickly.

3 If you had a _____ marrying for love or marrying for money, which would you do?

4 I know you have a cold, but that's no _____ not doing your homework.

5 If you have to deal with overseas clients, a _____ foreign languages is very useful.

6 Do you have any _____ my parking my car in front of your house?

7 Since the salmonella scare there has been a considerable _____ the consumption of eggs.

8 Perhaps the three most important human rights are _____ hunger, fear and persecution.

9 Einstein hated school and often missed classes, but he was a real _____ mathematics.

10 In the dispute between the union and the management, new
    proposals have been put forward which should at least provide a
    _____ discussion.

11 In our class, we can do as we like; our teacher has no
    _____ us at all.

12 The RSPCA is the Royal Society for the Prevention of
    _____ Animals.

13 Overweight people should not jog because it puts a great
    _____ their hearts.

14 The African elephant will be extinct within twenty years if an
    international _____ the ivory trade is not started
    immediately.

15 Vandalising public property is the only way some youngsters can
    express their _____ society.

You can often guess which preposition will follow the noun by the meaning
of the preposition itself. For example, a *campaign* could be a *campaign for*
something good (you are in favour of it), or a *campaign against* something
bad (you are opposed to it).

19 Compound prepositions 1

Complete the following prepositional phrases by choosing a word from the list below. When you have finished, try to make up a sentence using each of the phrases.

| ~~a cost~~ | agreement | answer | behalf | good terms | means | peace |
| pity | reference | the compliments | the benefit | the influence |

1	at _____*a cost*_____ of
2	at _____ with
3	by _____ of
4	for _____ of
5	in _____ with
6	in _____ to
7	on _____ of
8	on _____ with
9	out of _____ for
10	under _____ of
11	with _____ to
12	with _____ of

The most common preposition to be used after a noun is *of. Of* is used in many expressions of place, such as *at the top of, at the bottom of, at the side of, at the back of, in front of, in the centre of, in the middle of.*

20 Fill the gaps 2

Complete these sentences with the correct preposition.

1 Congratulations ___*on*___ your thirty-fifth birthday!

2 With reference _____ your advertisement in today's *Guardian*, I wish to apply for the position of Sales Manager.

3 We have a good working relationship _____ the local authority.

4 Do you take pride _____ your appearance, or are you just vain?

5 The party's new policy document puts a strong emphasis _____ public ownership of basic utilities like electricity and water.

6 John's got very strange taste _____ clothes, hasn't he?

7 There has been a considerable improvement _____ the flow of traffic since they opened the extra lanes on the motorway.

8 'Have you made proper provision _____ your old age?'
   'No, I intend to become a burden on my children!'

9 Let Alicia work it out; she has an amazing aptitude _____ figures.

10 If you put as much effort _____ your schoolwork as you do _____ roller-blading, you might have a chance.

11 In a surprising departure _____ tradition, the Queen rode to Parliament on a bicycle.

12 Football fans showed their disapproval _____ the referee's decision by booing loudly.

13 Please give my regards _____ your mother when you see her.

14 Extensive research _____ artificial sweeteners has shown that rats die quickly if you drop large blocks of saccharine on them!

15 Picking your nose in public is not illegal, but it is certainly an offence _____ good manners.

Compound prepositions are made of the pattern PREPOSITION + NOUN + PREPOSITION, e.g. *with reference to*. They are sometimes used where a single preposition would be enough:

I wish to talk to you
{
 with respect to
 in respect of
 in connection with
 about
}
your proposal.

21 Sentence transformation 3

For each of the sentences below use the noun in capital letters and a suitable preposition to write a new sentence. The new sentence should be as similar as possible in meaning to the original.

1 Are you and Jennifer related? **RELATIVE**
Are you ____*a relative of*____ Jennifer's?

2 Pay no attention to what he says. **NOTICE**
Take no _____ what he says.

3 People are demanding lower taxes. **REDUCTION**
People are demanding a _____
taxes.

4 My boss seems to enjoy humiliating people. **PLEASURE**
My boss seems to take _____
humiliating people.

5 The interview panel thought that Sarah had **IMPRESSION**
a very good manner.
Sarah made a good _____
the interview panel.

6 My best friend is someone I can really trust. **CONFIDENCE**
I really have _____ my
best friend.

7 Henry really knew how to make people laugh. **TALENT**
Henry had a _____ making
people laugh.

8 Many filmmakers were influenced by the film **IMPACT**
Citizen Kane.
The film *Citizen Kane* had an _____
many filmmakers.

9 This rule is always true.   EXCEPTIONS

There are no _____ this rule.

---

10 A lot more people are buying automatic cars   DEMAND
these days.

There is a greater _____
automatic cars these days.

---

11 Lloyds the butcher's and Lloyds Bank are   CONNECTION
two completely separate organizations.

There is no _____ Lloyds Bank
and Lloyds the butcher's.

---

12 Emma knows a great deal about organic farming.   EXPERT

Emma is an _____ organic farming.

Noun phrases are often associated with a particular verb. For example, if
you are proud of your appearance, you **take** pride in it; if you visit someone,
you **make** or **pay** a visit to them.

22 Fill the gaps 3

Complete these sentences with a suitable preposition.

1. Do you know of a cure ___*for*___ hiccups?

2. The public is taking a lot of interest _____ the new courses being offered by the university.

3. The attendance _____ Saturday's match was very poor.

4. Did he give you any reason _____ his awful behaviour?

5. 'Take advantage _____ this special offer! 50% off list price while stocks last!'

6. At school today, we had a long discussion _____ the best way to learn a foreign language.

7. There's a big difference between being fond of someone and being in love _____ them!

8. 'Because of a lack _____ interest, tomorrow has been cancelled.' (notice outside a theatre)

9. It's a pity _____ poor old Fred: everyone got a Christmas present except him.

10. There has been a sharp increase _____ house prices in recent months.

11. Competitors in the New York Marathon began to drop out of the race one _____ one.

12. There seems to be some confusion _____ what Nelson actually said as he lay dying. Was it 'Kiss me, Hardy' or 'Kismet, Hardy'?

13. Professor Jonah Newt is a specialist _____ marine biology.

14. Because of the increase in the number of firms offering financial services, there's a bigger demand than ever _____ qualified accountants.

15. If you want to know how to get into other people's computers, pay a visit _____ the website www.hackers.com!

23 Compound prepositions 2

Complete the prepositional phrases below by choosing a word from the following list. When you have finished, try to make up a sentence using each of the phrases.

> account   addition   common   ~~exchange~~   favour   odds   regard
> respect   the exception   the expense   the sake   virtue

1   in _____*exchange*_____ for

2   in _____ with

3   in _____ to

4   in _____ of

5   at _____ with

6   at _____ of

7   with _____ to

8   with _____ of

9   for _____ of

10 out of _____ for

11 on _____ of

12 by _____ of

With or without *the*?

Sometimes, the meaning changes depending on whether *the* is used or not, e.g. *in front of my house* and *in the front of the book* (the front page or front part of the book). In most cases it is a matter of learning the expression as a whole.

24 Noun + preposition crossword

Read through the sentences below and complete the crossword. Most of the missing words are either prepositions or nouns.

Across

4 There has been a sharp _____ in the number of people staying on at school over the age of sixteen. There are at least 25% more now than there were three years ago (8).

6 For this job you need to be fluent in French and have a good working knowledge _____ at least two other European languages (2).

8 She has a _____ for being very efficient and hard-working (10).

11 Don't _____ your bike out in the rain: it will get rusty! (5)

13 You shouldn't have any _____ in getting to know people in Ecuador. Everyone is so friendly there (10).

14 Being tall, Audrey had a definite advantage _____ others in the team (4).

16 My company will not do business _____ countries that use child labour (4).

18 '_____ on tight, the bus is about to move!' (4)

20 Fighting the threat of global pollution is a race _____ time (7).

21 Can I have the _____ for your fruit cake? (6)

24 '_____ me about your date with Dave. I want to hear ALL the details!' (4)

25 'To be or not to be' is a _____ from Hamlet (9).

Down

1 The letters RSPCA stand for the Royal Society for the Prevention of _____ to Animals (7).

2 Is there a great difference _____ British and American English? (7)

3 What is your attitude _____ people who break the speed limit? (7)

5 On her eighteenth birthday Linda's grandmother gave her a _____ for £1,000 (6).

7 Brazil is rich _____ natural resources (2).

9 Switch the light _____ : it's more fun in the dark! (3)

10 Does anyone here have a _____ to the problem? (8)

12   The verdict was death _____ natural causes (4).

15   I've just heard about Angela's _____ to Thomas. I wonder when the wedding will be? (10)

17   Since she was a mechanic, I asked for her _____ on buying a second-hand car (6).

19   See 23 down.

22   Is your brother still having treatment _____ asthma? (3)

23 , **19**   I _____ _____ a cat when I was driving to work this morning. I felt really bad about it (3, 4).

24   She is heir _____ the family fortune. That's probably why so many men would like to marry her (2).

Section 4:
Preposition + noun (1)

The pattern PREPOSITION + NOUN gives English many phrases which answer questions like 'Where?' 'When?' 'How?' and 'Why?', e.g. *in prison*, *at times*, *with difficulty*, *for fun*.

Where the noun has a general sense, *the* is not needed, e.g. he is *in prison* means he is a prisoner.

Where the noun refers to something specific, *the* is needed, e.g. he is *in **the** prison* means he is a visitor or an employee in a particular prison.

Tall people are definitely at an advantage at a football match.

25 Noun groups

Fill in the spaces by placing the following nouns under a suitable preposition (four under each). When you have finished, see if you can make up a sentence for each of these prepositional phrases.

a moment	accident	dawn	fact	~~first~~	future	heart	holiday
least	lunch	name	private	sale	Salvador Dali	schedule	strike

AT

first

_____

_____

_____

BY

_____

_____

_____

_____

IN

_____

_____

_____

_____

ON

_____

_____

_____

_____

Sometimes the same noun can take different prepositions, with a change of meaning. For example: _in time_ means _not too late_; **on** _time_ means _as scheduled_.

26 *On* + noun

Complete the boxes by filling in the gaps in the following sentences.

1 The soldiers had orders to shoot
the deserter on **_sight_** .

S	I	G	H	T

2 'On no _____ are you to accept
lifts from strangers,' parents tell
their children.

	C				T

3 We'd all better arrive on _____
tomorrow; otherwise we might
miss the train.

		M	

4 I see Marc's put his house on the
_____ . Mind you, I don't
think it'll be very easy to sell.

	A			

5 Don't you hate it when a
telephone operator puts you on
_____ ?

H			

6 Your book hasn't come yet. But
it's on _____, so it should arrive
by Friday.

O		E	

7 'You're going to go on a long
_____,' said the fortune-teller as I
fell out of the window.

O		R		

8 I've put on a lot of weight lately.
I think I'd better go on a _____
again.

			T

9 All Sarah's friends were busy, so she had to go to the party on her _____ .

		N

10 Tonight is important. So remember, be on your best _____ .

B			V			R

11 Before buying anything, it's a good idea to send for a sample on _____ .

	P	P		V	L

12 I hate planning things; it's much more fun to do everything on _____ .

I		P		S	

13 I never pay cash; I always get everything on _____ .

	R		D		T

14 The Marketing Manager isn't here this week. She's gone to Buenos Aires on _____ .

	S		N		S

15 Don't write to me between June 1st and the 16th as I shall be on _____ then.

	O		D		

The preposition *on* can be used for:

- time, e.g. *on* Friday morning;

- place, e.g. *on* the train;

- subject matter, e.g. The Director gave a talk *on* the pros and cons of e-commerce.

27 Jumbled sentences 1

In the following sentences, the nouns are in the wrong places. Put each one into the correct sentence.

1. My uncle is in (a) **FASHION** at the moment with a broken leg.

2. Although the patient was obviously in great (b) **LUXURY**, she never once complained.

3. The detective asked the witness to describe the scene of the crime in (c) **EXISTENCE**.

4. There are things you will do in private that you would never do in (d) **HOSPITAL**.

5. Paul can't concentrate on anything these days. He's in (e) **FOCUS** again, I'm afraid.

6. This is the only known copy of the book in (f) **GENERAL**. All the others were destroyed in a fire.

7. She told us that if we were ever in (g) **PUBLIC**, we could rely on her for help.

8. 'I'll overlook it this time,' said the teacher, 'but remember to do your homework in (h) **FACT**.'

9. Winning £2 million on the football pools made it possible for him to live in (i) **DETAIL** for the rest of his life.

10. He didn't want anyone to recognise him, so he went to the party in (j) **DOUBT**.

11. Are you sure the projector's in (k) **DIFFICULTY**? Everything looks very blurred to me.

12. Ask your solicitor if you're in (l) **PAIN** about anything in the contract.

13. I see short skirts are in (m) **DISGUISE** again.

14. In (n) **FUTURE**, cats are more independent than dogs.

15. I don't dislike classical music at all. In (o) **LOVE**, I often go to the Opera.

Write your answers here:

1	2	3	4	5	6	7	8	9	10	11	12	13	14	15
d														

The preposition *in* can be used in relation to:

- time, e.g. *in the morning*;

- space, e.g. *in another country*;

- manner (how something is done), e.g. *tell me in a few words about yourself*, or, *he replied in a really offensive way*.

28 At, by, in, on, out of

Complete the following sentences using *at, by, in, on* or *out of*.

1   Mum must be ___*in*___ a bad mood: she's just thrown Dad out of the window.

2   Do sit down. Ms Brown will join you _____ a moment.

3   *The Street Lawyer* is a novel _____ John Grisham.

4   The car went over the brow of the hill and was soon _____ sight.

5   If trains always leave _____ schedule, why do so many of them arrive late at the other end?

6   Could you come back in half an hour? Mr Williams is _____ lunch at the moment.

7   If you can't finish the report today, it must be done _____ the weekend at the latest.

8   The survivors of the *Titanic* were _____ sea for several days before being rescued.

9   Does it matter what politicians do _____ private as long as they behave well in their jobs?

10   'Would you like a drink, Officer?'
       'Not while I'm _____ duty, Sir.'

11   'Why have you got a pet buffalo in the house?'
       'I wanted something a little _____ the ordinary.'

12   I bought an old car cheaply, cleaned it up and sold it next day _____ a profit.

13   It's not like John to lose his temper. It's completely _____ character.

14   Most people would jump _____ the chance to spend a year in America, all expenses paid.

Out of can refer to:

- no longer having, e.g. **out of** *stock*, **out of** *breath*;
- the origin or material used, e.g. *made* **out of** *wood*;
- a motive or cause, e.g. *she acted* **out of** *spite*.

29 Against, at, off, on, under

Complete the following sentences using *against, at, off, on* or *under*.

1   Tall people are definitely **_at_** an advantage at a football match.

2   The last item _____ the agenda is 'any other business'.

3   When I met my husband, it was love _____ first sight. It was only later that I had second thoughts!

4   Did you know that in some countries it is _____ the law to set fire to the national flag?

5   You can go to the disco tonight _____ condition that you are home by twelve o'clock.

6   After the war, several people were tried for crimes _____ humanity.

7   What I am telling you is not official, it's _____ the record, so please don't quote me.

8   The proposal to build a sports stadium in the town is still _____ discussion.

9   You could tell _____ a glance that she was used to appearing on stage.

10   I was _____ the impression that you had to be twenty-one to vote in general elections.

11   All forms of travel are expensive nowadays, but, _____ balance, air travel offers the best value for money.

12   You look really _____ the weather. Are you ill?

13   'This part of the airbase is _____ limits to non-military personnel.'

14   When the offer of a free trip to Holland was made, John was very quick _____ the mark, and managed to get the first ticket.

15   '_____ no circumstances should you leave your luggage unattended.' (airport security announcement)

> The preposition *under* can refer to:
> * a lower position, especially vertically lower, e.g. *hide **under** the bed*, *go **under** a bridge*;
> * being short of/less than, e.g. *a pair of trainers for **under** $30*;
> * in the reign/administration of, e.g. *things were better **under** the last government*.

30 Matching pairs 3

Each of the words and phrases on the left can be associated with one of the prepositional phrases on the right. Try to match them up correctly.

1	at a restaurant	a	on strike
2	simultaneously	b	behind bars
3	Don't tell anyone else!	c	in agony
4	running late	d	at a moment's notice
5	industrial dispute	e	at daybreak
6	It's burning!	f	behind the times
7	too young	g	out of order
8	machine not working	h	behind schedule
9	a prisoner	i	in flames
10	learn a poem	j	between you and me
11	with very little warning	k	at the same time
12	very early in the morning	l	by heart
13	old-fashioned	m	under age
14	It really hurts!	n	on the menu

Write your answers here:

1	2	3	4	5	6	7	8	9	10	11	12	13	14
n													

The article *the* is used where the noun refers to something specific or known, e.g. *behind the times* (meaning the times we live in) or, *on the menu* (meaning the menu in this particular restaurant).

31 Similar, but different

The following sentences each contain a prepositional phrase which could easily be confused with others, e.g. *on time, in time, at a time, at times*. Choose which phrase fits the sentence. There is only one correct answer for each sentence.

1   I always keep a dictionary __*to*__ hand in case I come across a word I don't know.

    a)   by   (b))   to   c)   out of

2   The technicians have checked the sound equipment and report that everything is _____ order.

    a)   on   b)   by   c)   in

3   I tried to find someone to type up my essay for me, but _____ the end I had to do it myself.

    a)   in   b)   by   c)   to

4   I've found a great newsgroup devoted to ice hockey! I came across it _____ chance when I was surfing the Web the other night.

    a)   from   b)   out of   c)   by

5   Have you seen this morning's paper? There's a big picture of you _____ the front page!

    a)   at   b)   on   c)   in

6   I've taken this watch _____ pieces, and now I can't put it together again.

    a)   into   b)   to   c)   in

7   The lady at the check-in desk said 'Window or aisle?' _____, I *think* that's what she said.

    a)   At least   b)   At last   c)   At the least

8   If you want to be a professional spy, you have to learn to be very secretive. _____ all, you must learn to listen more and speak less.

    a)   In   b)   At   c)   Above

9   I have some important information for you, but I don't want to give it _____ the phone. Do you think we could meet somewhere?

    a)   by   b)   through   c)   over

10 'Is everything OK, nurse?'

'Don't worry, doctor! Everything's _____ control.'

a) under   b) in   c) on

11 'Do you agree?'

'_____ point, but I don't think you are completely right.'

a) To the   b) Up to a   c) On the

12 I never met Joe Louis, but he was a great boxer _____ .

a) by all accounts   b) on account   c) in the account

13 I know _____ experience that I do my best work early in the morning.

a) in   b) from   c) with

14 '_____ during the performance of this trick, ladies and gentlemen, do my hands actually leave my arms!'

a) On time   b) In no time   c) At no time

15 There is nothing illegal about my business dealings. Everything is strictly _____ board.

a) on   b) above   c) by the

16 The red light goes on outside the studio door to let people know that you are _____ air.

a) on the   b) in the   c) through the

17 I forgot to pack any food so we'll get something to eat _____ the way back.

a) in   b) on   c) over

All the prepositional phrases in this test exist, but only one fits each sentence. For example, to be **on** *the way* means to be travelling; to be **in** *the way* means to be where you are not wanted; **by** *the way* means *incidentally*. Only the context will tell you which to choose.

32 Proverbs and sayings

A Complete the common sayings and proverbs below. Choose from the following prepositions – some are used more than once.

against	before	between	from	in	into
on	out of	over	up	with	without

1 A bird ____*in*____ the hand is worth two ____*in*____ the bush.

2 It's like banging your head _____ a brick wall.

3 _____ the devil and the deep blue sea.

4 To have a card _____ your sleeve.

5 To have several irons _____ the fire.

6 An iron fist _____ a velvet glove.

7 It's no use crying _____ spilt milk.

8 To keep the wolf _____ the door.

9 To kill two birds _____ one stone.

10 To make a mountain _____ a molehill.

11 _____ sight, _____ mind.

12 _____ the frying pan and _____ the fire.

13 To put the cart _____ the horse.

14 The grass is always greener _____ the other side.

15 There's no smoke _____ fire.

B Now match the expressions you have made to the meanings below.

a To take advantage of one action to achieve something else as well. `9`

b To be surrounded by problems with no escape. ☐

c There must be some truth in even the most unlikely rumour. ☐

d This describes someone who is much tougher or stricter than they appear to be on the surface. ☐

e You can only be sure of what you have at the moment; you cannot be sure of something which you might get in the future. ☐

f To exaggerate or make a big fuss over something which is not very serious. ☐

g To do things in the wrong order. ☐

h In negotiations, to have something in reserve that you have not yet revealed. ☐

i To just manage to earn enough to live on. ☐

j To express the idea that all your efforts are getting you nowhere. ☐

k An expression which describes the way you no sooner get out of one difficulty than you find yourself in another that is just as bad or worse. ☐

l An expression which describes our tendency to believe that life would be better for us somewhere else. ☐

m An expression which describes how easily we forget people as soon as we are no longer with them. ☐

n To have a number of different interests. ☐

o This proverb advises you not to waste time regretting things which you cannot change. ☐

Section 5:
Preposition + noun (2)

Prepositions express relationships, and most prepositions can have several meanings. For example, *over* can refer to:

- to or in a higher position, especially vertically higher, e.g. *fly **over** the city, lean **over** the bridge*;

- in authority, e.g. '*Send her victorious … long to reign **over** us*' (from the British National Anthem);

- value, quantity, number, e.g. *It cost **over** ten million pesetas*;

- a period of time, e.g. *I'm going to be very busy **over** the next three months*;

- on or to the other side of, e.g. *My best friend lives **over** the road*;

- on account of, e.g. *She got very upset **over** her daughter's decision to drop out of school*;

- recovered from the effects of, e.g. *I had a bad cold, but I am **over** it now*.

For more information about the various meanings and uses of the common prepositions see the tips in Sections 4 and 5.

'Hands up all those in favour of going to the seaside for the day.'

33 *At + noun*

In the following sentences, the nouns are in the wrong places. Put each one into the correct sentence.

1 The car came round the corner at **(a) A DISCOUNT**.

2 I'm not sure how old you are, but at **(b) YOUR OWN RISK**, I'd say you were about 110.

3 He was a very good shot and could hit a target at **(c) A DISADVANTAGE** of 300 metres.

4 We decided to leave at **(d) FIRST HAND** in order to get there before midday.

5 He was very reluctant to do it at **(e) LEAST**, but in the end he agreed.

6 Although we had not met before, my host soon made me feel completely at **(f) WAR**.

7 Despite what people might hope, women are still at **(g) NIGHT** when it comes to getting top jobs.

8 The normal price of the DVD was £225, but since business was slow, the Manager decided to sell them at **(h) A DISTANCE**.

9 Working in a bank isn't the most exciting job in the world perhaps, but at **(i) SHORT NOTICE** it pays the rent.

10 Don't worry about vampires. They sleep during the day and only come out at **(j) THE MOMENT**.

11 Between 1939 and 1945, Britain was at **(k) HOME** with Germany.

12 Tell us what you need in good time, please. We don't like doing things at **(l) A GUESS**.

13 I'm afraid the Director isn't here at **(m) FIRST**. Could you call back later?

14 There's a large notice in the school cloakroom which says: 'Coats are left here at **(n) DAWN.'**

15 I decided to go out to India to experience at **(o) FULL SPEED** the Indian way of life.

Write your answers here:

1	2	3	4	5	6	7	8	9	10	11	12	13	14	15
o														

The preposition *at* can refer to:
- time, e.g. *at ten o'clock*;
- space, e.g. *at school, arrival at the airport*;
- reaction, e.g. *surprised at, amazed at*;
- level of ability, e.g. *good at games*;
- activity, e.g. *He's at it again, mother!*;
- measurement, e.g. *three at a time, priced at 350 pesos*.

34 By + noun

Complete the boxes with the missing word from the following sentences.

1. I'd hate to go from England to Australia by _boat_ . Just imagine being seasick for six weeks!

B	O	A	T

2. By the _____ , my name's James Samuels. I'm Ms Thompson's assistant.

		Y

3. Probably the quickest way of travelling is by _____ .

A		

4. Fewer and fewer people pay cash nowadays; most pay by credit card or by _____ .

	H		U	

5. All public buildings are now required by _____ to have fireproof doors.

		W

6. Can you read music, or do you play by _____ ?

E		

7. I'm sorry, but Dr Salmon sees patients by _____ only.

	P	P			T			

8. By all _____ bring your boyfriend with you to the party on Saturday.

	E		S

9. Have you noticed how many politicians are lawyers by _____ ?

			F		S			

10 People who are shy and retiring by
_____ usually avoid being the
centre of attention.

| | | T | | | E |

---

11 The announcement that we could
have Friday off took us all by

_____ .

| | U | | P | | | |

---

12 My cousin is related to the
Governor by _____ . Her
husband is the Governor's brother.

| | | R | R | | | |

---

13 As the troublemakers wouldn't leave the
disco peacefully, they had to be removed
by _____ .

| | | R | | |

---

14 My father was a very private
person. I only found out by
_____ that he had been a pop
star in his youth.

| | C | C | | | | |

The preposition *by* can refer to:
- time, e.g. *by 7.30* (meaning, *not later than 7.30*);
- how something is made or done, e.g. *go **by** car, leave **by** the back door, made **by** hand*;
- authorship, e.g. The Rainmaker *is a novel **by** John Grisham*.

35 Preposition + noun pairs

Choose the best alternative to complete each of the following sentences.

1   Hands up all those (*in favour of*/*in favour with*) going to the seaside for the day.

2   Do you remember that scene (*at the end*/*in the end*) of the movie where Hugh Grant and Julia Roberts have a terrible argument?

3   When I was a teacher I knew all my pupils (*by name*/*in name*).

4   Who's that standing (*at the front of*/*in front of*) Claire in the photo?

5   (*In view of*/*With a view to*) the fact that only three people have signed up for Friday's concert, I'm afraid we'll have to cancel it.

6   I know them both (*by sight*/*on sight*), but I've no idea what their names are.

7   We were just (*in time*/*on time*) to see the Queen arrive at the theatre.

8   (*In case of*/*In the case of*) difficulty, you can reach me at this number.

9   He may seem tough and ruthless, but (*by heart*/*at heart*) he's a kind and gentle man.

10   You know you can always come to me (*at the time of*/*in time of*) need.

11   A mother gave her three children a bar of chocolate and told them to (*divide it between*/*divide it among*) themselves.

12   The proposal was accepted (*on principle*/*in principle*), but we asked for further details before making a final decision.

13   He never travelled abroad (*for fear of*/*in fear of*) becoming ill through eating foreign food.

14   These paintings have been (*in possession of*/*in the possession of*) my family for generations.

Between or among?

The word *between* comes from the same root as the word *two* and it refers strictly to two people, groups or things, e.g. **between** *you and me*, or, *Share the food equally* **between** *the boys and the girls*.

Among (or *amongst*) refers to more than two people, things or sets, e.g. *Talk* **amongst** *yourselves while I find the right page.*

36 Matching pairs 4

Each of the words and phrases on the left can be associated with one of the prepositional phrases on the right. Try to match them up correctly.

1	What a mess!	**a**	off form
2	I haven't eaten!	**b**	in disorder
3	Her husband just died.	**c**	in the flesh
4	a personal appearance	**d**	on an empty stomach
5	I can't pay!	**e**	in demand
6	very fashionable	**f**	under lock and key
7	She's winning!	**g**	in vogue
8	The picture is blurred.	**h**	in orbit
9	a satellite	**i**	in hiding
10	Your valuables are safe!	**j**	on the air
11	a radio broadcast	**k**	by degrees
12	a fugitive	**l**	in the lead
13	not playing well	**m**	in debt
14	very popular	**n**	out of focus
15	gradually	**o**	in mourning

Write your answers here:

1	2	3	4	5	6	7	8	9	10	11	12	13	14	15
b														

Off can refer to:

- movement or rest away from a place, e.g. *The glass rolled* **off** *the shelf, Keep* **off** *the grass*;
- opening out of, e.g. *the dining room is just* **off** *the main corridor*;
- disengaged from, e.g. *I am still a member of the club, but I am* **off** *the committee*;
- to have lost your appetite for something, e.g. *The poor old dog is* **off** *his food.*

37 *In* + noun

Complete the boxes on the right by filling in the gaps in the following sentences.

1. On really warm summer evenings, we usually have a barbecue in the __garden__ .

G	A	R	D	E	N

2. I always have a lie-in on Sunday mornings. I usually stay in _____ until 12 o'clock.

	E	

3. I can't stop, I'm afraid. I'm in a _____ .

				Y

4. I'm afraid the bank can't lend you more money, Mr Jarvis. You're already over £800 in _____ .

D		B	

5. This car may be old, but it's still in very good _____ .

			D		T		

6. All school fees must be paid in _____ .

A		V			C	

7. You'd better take some extra money with you in _____ you need to take a taxi home.

	A		

8. The secret service warned the President that her life would be in _____ if she carried out her plan to visit the war zone.

			G		R

9. Keep away from Simon; he's in a really bad _____ this morning.

		O	

10 In an _____ , dial 999
for the police, fire brigade or
ambulance service.

	M		R				Y

11 That joke was in very bad _____ .
You should be ashamed of yourself.

	T			

12 To prevent others from reading their messages,
the rebels communicated with each other in

_____ .

		D	

13 What I'm about to tell you
is in _____ , so
please don't say anything
to anyone else.

C			F					C	

14 'In _____ , may I
say how grateful I am to
everyone for making today
such a big success.'

C		N		L				N

15 There's nothing wrong
with playing computer
games as long as it's done
in _____ .

		D		R		T			

In or into?

In is the general word for movement or rest, e.g. *Go in the house! Stay in the classroom!*

Into refers to movement and is more precise. *Into* can refer to:

- movement to a position where you will be in(side), e.g. *We drove into Spain* (meaning out of another country and into Spain);
- in contact or collision with, e.g. *I swerved and ran into a lamppost*;
- enthusiasm for, e.g. *I am really into computer games.*

38 Sentence transformation 4

For each of the sentences below, use the noun in capital letters and a suitable prepositions to write a new sentence. The new sentence should be as similar as possible in meaning to the original.

1   I can recite Wordsworth's 'Prelude' without looking at the book.   MEMORY

I can recite Wordsworth's 'Prelude' *from memory* .

2   My bank manager and I get on together very well.   GOOD TERMS

My bank manager and I are _____ .

3   They got married without telling anyone.   SECRET

They got married _____ .

4   My grandfather was ninety-six when he died.   AGE

My grandfather died at the _____ ninety-six.

5   We live just outside the town.   OUTSKIRTS

We live on the _____ the town.

6   I don't feel like going out tonight.   MOOD

I'm not in the _____ going out tonight.

7   She spent the evening alone.   HERSELF

She spent the evening _____ .

8   I don't usually give lifts to hitch-hikers.   HABIT

I'm not in the _____ giving lifts to hitch-hikers.

9   We have run out of the items you want.   STOCK

The items you want are _____ .

---

10   The way to get the best out of me is to make me   PRESSURE
work very hard.

I work best _____ .

---

11   She attacked the intruder, but only to protect   SELF-DEFENCE
herself.

She attacked the intruder _____ .

---

12   I will finish work early today if everything goes well.   LUCK

I will finish work early today _____ any _____ .

---

13   We have decided to stay here permanently.   GOOD

We have decided to stay here _____ .

---

14   I accidentally pressed the 'eject' button.   MISTAKE

I pressed the 'eject' button _____ .

---

39 *After, at, for, in, to*

Complete the following sentences using *after*, *at*, *for*, *in* or *to*.

1 'Are all the preparations made?'

'Don't worry, everything is __*in*__ hand.'

2 You can change your job, you can move house, but marriage is meant to be _____ life.

3 Please, Dad, can I go to the cinema with Angela tonight? _____ all, I am thirty-three years old now!

4 We didn't know _____ certain whether they would come or not.

5 She told him _____ his face exactly what she thought of him.

6 Marianne is the sort of person who makes you feel immediately _____ ease.

7 There was a lot of excitement in class _____ the announcement that our teacher is moving to another school.

8 This is supposed to be a democracy, but it is a democracy _____ name only.

9 The clock is to be sold _____ auction.

10 My husband brought me some flowers today. He must be _____ something!

11 Tom sent a copy of his will to his bank _____ safe keeping.

12 We don't like the seaside much, but we usually take our holidays there _____ the children's sake.

13 _____ careful consideration, the government has decided not to put up the price of ice cream.

14 I'm sorry, but I'm not _____ liberty to tell you any more.

After can refer to:
- later in time, e.g. *Let's meet **after** school*;
- behind in place, e.g. *Why does B come **after** A in the alphabet?*;
- in honour of, e.g. *Armstrong Avenue is named **after** the first man to set foot on the moon*;
- following, e.g. *I think Maria is **after** me!*

40 Cartoon time 1

Match the captions to the cartoons, adding the missing prepositions.

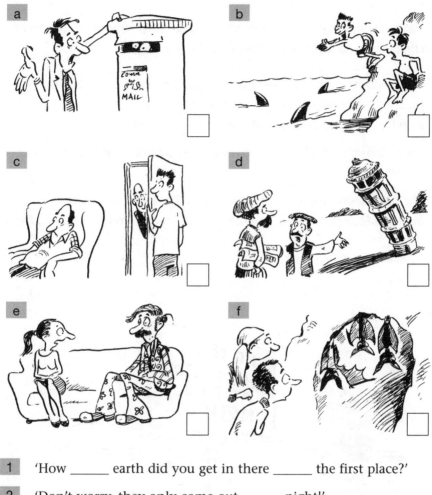

1 'How _____ earth did you get in there _____ the first place?'

2 'Don't worry, they only come out _____ night!'

3 'Well, if you wait long enough, they might come back _____ fashion, I suppose.'

4 '_____ second thoughts, I'll just stay here and watch.'

5 'Dad, there's a man _____ the door with a bald head.'
'Tell him I've already got one.'

6 'I didn't do it _____ purpose, honestly!'

Section 6:
Adjective + preposition

The most frequently used prepositions after adjectives are *to*, *of* and *for*. Others are *at*, *with*, *in*, *by*, *about*, *from* and *on*.

To help you remember which preposition to use, think about the meaning of the preposition as well as the meaning of the adjective.

- The preposition *with*, for example, describes the cause or instrument e.g., *He cut the loaf **with** a knife*. So, the use of *with* after *angry*, e.g. *I was angry **with** him*, is logical because he was the cause of my anger.

- The preposition *at* refers to ability, which explains *good **at** sports*, *bad **at** remembering things*, *quick **at** figures*.

- The preposition *from* refers to separation or absence, so it is logical to use *from* in adjectival phrases like *missing **from**, exempt **from**, disqualified **from***.

I once saw a notice that said, 'Do not throw stones at this notice'.

41 Adjective groups

Fill in the spaces below by placing the following adjectives under a suitable preposition (four under each). When you have finished, see if you can make up sentences containing each of the adjectival phrases.

according	accustomed	annoyed	aware	famous	friendly
handy	~~hopeless~~	jealous	late	opposed	pleased	popular
quick	ready	regardless	short	similar	surprised	valued

AT

hopeless

_____

_____

_____

OF

_____

_____

_____

_____

FOR

_____

_____

_____

_____

TO

_____

_____

_____

_____

WITH

_____

_____

_____

_____

42 Sentence transformation 5

For each of the sentences below, use the adjective in capital letters with a suitable preposition to write a new sentence. The new sentence should be as similar as possible in meaning to the original.

1   My father has always liked football.   INTERESTED

   My father has always been *interested in*
   football.

2   Everyone has heard about the leaning tower of Pisa.   FAMOUS

   Pisa is _____ its leaning tower.

3   We didn't think she would pass the exam.   DOUBTFUL

   We were _____ her passing the exam.

4   The painting is worth £25,000.   VALUED

   The painting is _____ £25,000.

5   This passport can be used in most countries.   VALID

   This passport is _____ most countries.

6   It's very easy to get to the station from my house.   HANDY

   My house is _____ the station.

7   Your car is like one I used to own.   SIMILAR

   I used to own a car _____ yours.

8   He would never tell you a lie.   INCAPABLE

   He is _____ telling a lie.

9 Sports cars are John's great passion. CRAZY

John is _____ sports cars.

10 It was very kind of you to help me. GRATEFUL

I am _____ you for your help.

11 All the teachers like Kate. POPULAR

Kate is _____ all the teachers.

12 The people of Dolichorhinia are noted for their long noses. CHARACTERISTIC

Long noses are _____ the people of Dolichorhinia.

13 There are saguaro cacti everywhere in the deserts of South Arizona. TYPICAL

Saguaro cacti are _____ the deserts of South Arizona.

14 I have never seen this kind of mountain bike before. NEW

This kind of mountain bike is _____ me.

Where there are two objects, they usually take different prepositions, e.g.
*I am grateful **to** you **for** coming*, or, *The painting was valued **by** the expert **at** $20,000.*

43 Complete the sentences 3

Complete the sentences below with one of the following adjectives plus a preposition.

> allergic deep distracted envious exempt fortunate
> quick sensitive suited ~~sympathetic~~ unaware

---

1 Although they said they were __*sympathetic to*__ our cause, they were not prepared to support us officially.

2 Sarah was very _____ figures, so she eventually became a successful accountant.

3 I am _____ anyone who can play the piano really well. When it comes to keyboards, I have five thumbs on each hand!

4 Most people are _____ the difference between Eskimo and Inuit.

5 Some plants are so _____ pollution that they can only survive in a perfectly clean environment.

6 Newton, the discoverer of gravity, was so _____ thought one morning that his housekeeper found him holding an egg in his hand, having dropped his watch into the boiling water.

7 The flat wasn't very big, but it was perfectly _____ our needs.

8 Candidates with university degrees are _____ parts I and II of the examination.

9 Charles is disabled, so he is _____ having a wife who is also a trained nurse.

10 I don't like open-plan offices. I am too easily _____ other people's phones.

11 I am _____ animal fur, so I avoid visiting friends who have cats or dogs in the house.

Is *to* part of the adjective phrase or part of the verb?
Distinguish between the pattern adjective + *to* + the *-ing* form of the verb, e.g.
*The secretary's duties are **limited to taking** notes at Board meetings*, and the
pattern adjective + infinitive with *to*, e.g. *I am very **happy to see** you again.*

44 About, at, by, for, in, of, on, with

Complete the following sentences using *about*, *at*, *by*, *for*, *in*, *of*, *on*, or *with*.

1   I once saw a notice that said: *'Do not throw stones __at__ this notice'*.

2   I am astonished _____ the way my students can spend all night at the disco and still make it into class the next morning.

3   There's no point in getting upset _____ things which are beyond your control.

4   I am a bit weak _____ science subjects, but I am trying to improve.

5   Are you familiar _____ Professor Wilhelm's work on bilingualism in parrots?

6   Susan is disabled but she likes to do things for herself. She hates to be dependent _____ others.

7   Don't you get annoyed _____ people who push past you without saying 'Excuse me'?

8   Sorry I'm late! I was so absorbed _____ my book, I didn't realize what time it was.

9   That's no way to behave! You ought to be ashamed _____ yourself!

10   I wonder who is responsible _____ all that amazing graffiti you see on public buildings?

11   Sarah is studying hard. She is intent _____ getting a good degree.

12   That remark was not worthy _____ you.

Sometimes more than one preposition can be used with little or no change of meaning, e.g. *upset **about** something* and *upset **over** something* mean the same thing; or *annoyed **at** someone* and *annoyed **with** someone* mean the same.

45 Sentence transformation 6

For each of the sentences below use the adjective in capital letters with a suitable preposition to rewrite the sentence. The new sentence should be as similar as possible in meaning to the original.

1 The Health and Safety Act forbids smoking in restaurant kitchens.   CONTRARY

Smoking is ___*contrary to*___ the Health and Safety Act.

---

2 The library has lost a number of books lately.   MISSING

A number of books are _____ the library.

---

3 I did not like the way you spoke to your sister.   DISGUSTED

I was _____ the way you spoke to your sister.

---

4 Do you know the works of the poet William Macgonagall?   FAMILIAR

Are you _____ the works of William Macgonagall?

---

5 We have scarcely enough money to live on.   SHORT

We are very _____ money.

---

6 Our customs and theirs are not the same.   DIFFERENT

Their customs are _____ ours.

---

7 You and I have exactly the same earrings.   IDENTICAL

Your earrings are _____ mine.

---

8 Polar bears are found only in the Arctic regions.   PECULIAR

Polar bears are _____ the Arctic regions.

---

9 We may have to increase our prices without warning.　　SUBJECT

Our prices are _____ increase without
warning.

10 People associate Oscar Wilde with wit.　　WELL KNOWN

Oscar Wilde is _____ his wit.

11 Julie loves jazz; she listens to it all the time.　　MAD

Julie is _____ jazz.

12 The latest opinion poll suggests that fewer
people eat meat nowadays compared to
twenty years ago.　　ACCORDING

_____ the latest opinion poll,
fewer people eat meat nowadays.

13 Bad weather over the Atlantic caused the delay to
our flight.　　DUE

The delay to our flight was _____ bad
weather over the Atlantic.

14 A new DVD player was just what Jack wanted.　　DELIGHTED

Jack was _____ his new DVD player.

Different from or different to?

Languages change over time. Purists still insist that *different **from*** is correct,
but many people now say *different **to***.

46 Complete the sentences 4

Complete the sentences below with one of the following adjectives plus a preposition.

> addicted   angry   ~~bad~~   based   capable   disqualified   expert
> famous   followed   full   involved   jealous   surprised

1 Don't ask me to add up the bill. I'm really ___*bad at*___ maths.

2 Although Tony wouldn't admit it, everyone could see that he was _____ his brother's success.

3 Some people become so _____ the Internet that they spend all night surfing the Web.

4 Janet! I'm _____ you playing computer games when you are supposed to be working!

5 The city of Sydney is _____ its wonderful Opera House, amongst other things.

6 The musical *West Side Story* was _____ Shakespeare's *Romeo and Juliet*.

7 For dinner we had grilled fish and vegetables, _____ a huge serving of strawberries and cream.

8 Teachers soon get _____ their students if they don't do their homework.

9 'We know you weren't alone, Biggs,' the detective said, 'so, who else was _____ the crime?'

10 Life is _____ surprises, isn't it?

11 I know how to use the Internet, but I wouldn't say I was _____ it.

12 Lately, several athletes have been _____ taking part in their events because they failed their drug tests.

13 'Do you think politicians are _____ telling lies?'

'Everybody is!'

> Sometimes different prepositions can be used after an adjective, depending on the meaning, e.g. you say *to be angry **about** something*, but, *to be angry **with** somebody*.

47 Find the missing adjective

Match each phrase on the left (1–14) with a phrase on the right (a–n) and put in the missing adjective. Choose from the following.

> accompanied ~~accustomed~~ blind convenient due hopeless keen
> late nervous opposed pleased regardless rich suspicious

1 She's a farmer's daughter, so she is
accustomed

a ... for the motorway.

b ... of strangers.

2 Harry's so slow, he'll even be _____

c ... to working with animals.

3 This car has high mileage and is
_____

4 She didn't like the jacket but she was
_____

d ... of gender, age or ethnic origin.

5 I don't like rap music, but I am
_____

e ... with the skirt.

6 The examination wasn't difficult, but I'm _____

f ... to his weaknesses.

7 She's good at languages, but _____

g ... about the results.

8 I'm in favour of fishing, but _____

h ... by an adult.

9 The job is open to all, _____

i ... on salsa.

10 The house is outside town, but is
_____

j ... for his own funeral!

11 He lives alone in a remote village, so is
_____

k ... in other minerals.

12 No children are admitted unless
_____

l ... to hunting.

13 It's a country without much oil, but
_____

m ... for a service.

n ... at maths and science.

14 He knows his good points, but he's
_____

Remember: some adjectives may be followed by a preposition or by the infinitive with *to*, depending on meaning, e.g. *He was pleased **with** his present*, and, *Pleased **to meet** you*; or *I'm keen **on** horse racing*, and, *I'm keen **to learn** karate*.

48 Adjective + preposition crossword

Read through the sentences below and complete the crossword. The missing words are either adjectives or prepositions.

Across

2 We're having a party on Saturday and I'm really excited _____ it (5).

3 Everyone thought John would stay single, so we were really surprised when we heard that he had got _____ to a Swedish girl (7).

4 At first Pierre found it quite difficult to drive in Britain because he was not _____ to driving on the left (10).

8 Everyone felt _____ for him because he didn't pass his exams (5).

9 Peter has always been _____ of the dark, and that's why he sleeps with the lights on (6).

11 I'm not very _____ at tennis; I always seem to lose (4).

12 What a saleswoman! She's _____ in all her business deals. She hasn't once failed to get an order (10).

14 If you're not _____ with the service at the hotel, then you should complain to the manager (9).

18 My sister doesn't think that guns are very _____ toys for children. If she had her way, they'd all be banned (8).

19 The boss has been ill _____ a cold for the past week (4).

Down

1 You are not allowed to be _____ from school without permission (6).

5 When the children woke up on Christmas morning they were excited to see the ground _____ with snow (7).

6 She was so _____ in her newspaper that she didn't notice me come in (9).

7 James is late again! That's _____ of him! I don't think he's ever been early for anything in his entire life! (7)

10 Looking at the way Dave dances, I see what Darwin meant when he said that we were _____ from apes (9).

11 I am very _____ to you for all your help (8).

13 My sister is _____ in French and German and also has a reasonable working knowledge of Spanish and Italian (6).

15 I'm _____ of eating potatoes every day. Why can't we have rice for a change? (5)

16 The Galapagos Islands are _____ for their amazing wildlife (6).

17 The man was found _____ of the crime and sentenced to four years' imprisonment (6).

Section 7:
Prepositions in context

This section tests:

Your knowledge of all the different uses of prepositions:
- movement and rest in space, e.g. *into the sea, under the table*
- points in and duration of time, e.g. *on Friday, for ages*
- purpose, e.g. *ready for bed*
- cause, e.g. *suffer from asthma*
- emotion, e.g. *surprised at someone*
- method, e.g. *travel by bus*

All the patterns of prepositional phrases:
- adjective + preposition, e.g. *jealous of*
- verb + preposition, e.g. *remind someone of something*
- verb + adverb + preposition, e.g. *make up for*
- noun + preposition, e.g. *thanks to*
- preposition + noun, e.g. *in theory*

Examples of compound phrases:
- verb + noun + preposition, e.g. *play tricks on*
- verb + preposition + noun, e.g. *go into business*
- preposition + noun + preposition, e.g. *for the sake of*

Prepositional phrases used in idiomatic phrases, e.g. *once in a blue moon*

She's very busy at the moment; she's up to her eyeballs in work.

49 Holiday disaster

Read through the following and fill in the numbered blanks with **one** suitable preposition.

(1) _____ a camping holiday (2) _____ Spain, our pet dog Betsy, who had been brought along (3) _____ the sake of the children, died suddenly (4) _____ the night.

The children said that we simply couldn't bury the poor animal (5)_____ a foreign country, where we might never be able to visit her grave again, so we decided to head (6) _____ home and attempt to smuggle her (7) _____ Spain and France and so back (8)_____ England.

With this (9) _____ mind, we rolled Betsy's body (10) _____ a carpet, tied it on to the roof rack (11) _____ the car along (12) _____ the camping equipment and started off (13) _____ our journey.

We drove (14) _____ the night without stopping and heaved a sigh of relief as we crossed the border out of Spain and (15) _____ France.

(16) _____ this time all the family were very tired and hungry, so we decided to stop (17) _____ breakfast. We parked the car (18) _____ a side street (19) _____ to a suitable café. Not wanting to leave poor Betsy (20) _____ too long, we ate a quick breakfast and returned (21) _____ the car. However, (22) _____ our horror, all our possessions had been stolen (23) _____ the roof of the car, including the carpet containing our pet's body!

50 Old friends

A Paul has written to an old friend, Bob. Here is his letter, but the pieces are mixed up. Try to put them in order. Label the pieces 1–9.

a
> ... in the summer.
> Give my regards to your parents and write soon.
> Lots of love
> Paul

[ ]

b
> ... near Hastings. They thought you might like to join us for two weeks – from 2–15 August. It sleeps four, so there's plenty of room. And it's only five minutes ...

[ ]

c
> ... out if your parents received the holiday brochures he sent, as he hasn't heard ...

[ ]

d
> ... in the summer. Mum and Dad have rented a caravan in Fairlight – a little village ...

[ ]

e
> Dear Bob,
> Sorry I've taken such a long time in answering your letter. The truth is that I've been really busy these past few weeks ...

[1]

f
> ... from the sea, so we could go swimming every day. It should be great fun, but it would be even better if you could be there too. So what do you say? Apart ...

[ ]

g
> ... from them yet.
> Well, Bob, that's all for now. I hope you're keeping well and that you'll be able to join us ...

[ ]

h
> ... from this, there's not much to say really. Dad's got a new car – a Volvo – and Mum's just started back to work again.
> By the way, Dad asked me to find ...

[ ]

i
> ... with exams and everything. I hope you understand.
> My main reason for writing is to ask if you'd like to spend a couple of weeks with us ...

[ ]

B Here is Bob's reply. Again, put the pieces in the correct order. Label
them 1–10.

a
> ... to your Mum and Dad.
> Lots of love
> Bob

☐

b
> ... of things to do – especially in the summer. So thank your parents
> for me and tell them I'm really looking forward to it.
> I asked Mum and Dad ...

☐

c
> ... course I'd love to join you and your parents in Fairlight. It sounds
> really fun. I visited Hastings once and it was a really nice place – lots ...

☐

d
> ... for almost three months (not bad for me!). What about you? Are you
> still going out with Pauline or have you got someone new now?
> Anyway, do write some time and remember to give my love ...

☐

e
> ... of the new Volvo. He's always liked foreign cars – especially
> Volvos – and keeps hinting ...

☐

f
> ... with Sally. You remember Sally, don't you? She was the girl I met
> at Jenny's birthday party. We've been together now ...

☐

g
> Dear Paul
> Many thanks for your letter. It was good to hear from you at last
> (I was beginning to think you had emigrated or something!).
> About the summer, yes, of ...

1

h
> ... for all the trouble he's gone to.
> By the way, Paul, Dad's very jealous ...

☐

i
> ... to Mum about getting a new car. But she's not interested
> really, so I don't think he'll persuade her.
> Well, Paul, I'll stop now because I'm off to a disco ...

☐

j
> ... about the holiday brochures. They haven't received them yet
> (you know what the post is like!). But they'll write as soon as they
> get them, and they asked me to tell you to thank your Dad ...

☐

When you do this kind of exercise, look at the words at the beginning and
end of each segment to see what will match up. For example, you know the
expression *to thank someone for something* – one segment ends in the words
thank your Dad ... which tells you to look for a segment beginning with *for* ...

51 Jumbled sentences 2

In the following sentences, the prepositional phrases are all in the wrong place. Put each one into the correct sentence.

1   I don't mind a bit of fun, but putting salt in Gran's coffee is
    (a) OUT OF DATE.

2   How long can you stay **(b) IN BLOSSOM** before you have to come up
    for air?

3   John is in Saudi Arabia **(c) WITH CARE**, but he should be home next
    week.

4   Before we were married, you said that you would love me
    (d) ON MY KNEES.

5   The idea looks good **(e) IN GEAR**, but will it really work?

6   The parcel which the postman threw on to my desk has 'Fragile,
    handle **(f) FOR EVER'** written on it.

7   The orchard is beautiful in spring, when all the fruit trees are
    (g) OUT OF THE QUESTION.

8   I can see from your tie that you had a boiled egg **(h) AT PRESENT.**

9   When I went down **(i) AFTER DARK** and asked her to marry me, she
    said I was not tall enough.

10 I didn't get a pay rise: the boss said that it was **(j) ON PAPER** this
    year.

11 Practical training is often known as **(k) BEYOND A JOKE** training.

12 This encyclopedia is **(l) UNDER ARREST**: it says that the present
    ruler of France is Napoleon Bonaparte.

13 When the police told him he was **(m) ON THE JOB** for speeding, my
    grandfather was amazed, as he was on his bicycle at the time.

14 The park is safe during the day, but you should not go there alone
    (n) FOR BREAKFAST.

15 When you park, don't just put on the handbrake. Leave the car **(o)**
    UNDER WATER as well.

Write your answers here:

1	2	3	4	5	6	7	8	9	10	11	12	13	14	15
k														

52 Audrey Hepburn

Read through the following and fill in the numbered blanks with a suitable preposition.

Audrey Hepburn was born in 1930 (1) __*in*__ Belgium. (2) _____ the age of seventeen, she won a scholarship to study ballet in London. Not very long (3) _____ that, she found herself playing small parts (4) _____ English screen comedies. Her performance in a movie called *Monte Carlo Baby* brought her (5) _____ the attention of director William Wyler, who had no doubt (6) _____ her talent. Thanks (7) _____ him, she was an instant success: when she was only twenty-four, she won an Oscar (8) _____ her first starring role.

For the next fifteen years, she worked (9) _____ Hollywood's most famous directors such as William Wyler and Billy Wilder. She played (10) _____ giants of the screen like Humphrey Bogart, Henry Fonda and Fred Astaire in many movies, (11) _____ which *My Fair Lady* and *Breakfast at Tiffany's* are perhaps the best known.

She stayed away (12) _____ the cameras for nine years (13) _____ order to raise her two sons. In 1976, she returned (14) _____ the silver screen and worked in two films before making her final appearance as an angel in Steven Spielberg's *Always*.

(15) _____ addition (16) _____ her success on screen, she tirelessly devoted herself (17) _____ her work as an ambassador for UNICEF. Her trip (18) _____ Somalia helped focus the world's attention (19) _____ that tragic land. Her dedication (20) _____ the cause of suffering children came (21) _____ personal experience: during the Second World War, as a young teenager in the Nazi-occupied Netherlands, Hepburn and her mother had survived (22) _____ eating tulip bulbs.

In January 1993, she died (23) _____ cancer (24) _____ her home (25) _____ Switzerland.

Tell me and **explain to me**.

Verbs like *tell me* include *advise*, *inform*, *show*, *teach*.

Verbs like *explain to me* include *demonstrate*, *mention*, *point out*, *prove*, *report*.

53 How was your holiday?

A Pauline Wood has just returned from a holiday in Spain. She has written to her travel agent, Sunthorn Holidays, about the holiday. Put the letter in the correct order. Label the pieces 1–13. How was her holiday? Why?

a
... for a seat next to the window.
   This is the worst holiday I have ever had in my life, and I demand my money back. If not, I shall put the matter in the hands of my solicitor. I look forward ...

b
... in an aisle seat despite the fact that I had specifically asked ...

c
... on the first plane so that there was a further delay in ...

d
Dear Sir,
I have just returned from a holiday in Spain and all I can say is that it was a nightmare from ...

1

e
... our departure. To begin with, the plane was overbooked. This meant that myself and ten other passengers were forced to go on another plane – one hour later! Unfortunately, our luggage was still ...

f
... to hearing from you soon.
Yours faithfully
Pauline Wood

g
... construction, which meant that there was the constant sound of cement mixers – hardly the peaceful and relaxing holiday I had been looking forward to. My room was much smaller than I had expected and throughout ...

h
... the sea. Twenty-five to be exact! And what a beach! It was so polluted that it was positively dangerous ...

80   Section 7: Prepositions in context

i ... with a company I could rely on. How wrong could I have been?
The trouble started even before ...

j ... sorting out the mess when we finally arrived at the airport in Spain.
The 'luxury' hotel as advertised in your holiday brochure was still under ...

k ... to one's health.
Finally, on the return journey, I was made to sit ...

l ... start to finish! When I chose Sunthorn Holidays, I was under the
impression that I was dealing ...

m ... my stay, I never once managed to get the shower to work properly – the
water was either too hot or too cold.
Another thing: in your brochure you state that the hotel is only a few
minutes from ...

B Here's a letter from another client of Sunthorn Holidays. Again, put the
pieces in the correct order. Label them 1–11. What did Bernard Wilson
think of his holiday?

a ... future that all 'extra' costs are clearly shown in your brochure.
Apart ...

b ... for separately! Unfortunately, our travel representative forgot to mention
this fact until we were well at sea! By ...

c ... from the above, the rest of our holiday in Copenhagen was wonderful,
and both my wife and I fell in love ...

d ... of the city. Whatever happens, we shall certainly return to Copenhagen at ...

e ... from Sunthorn Holidays, the holiday was to include a two-day boat trip
to Oslo in ...

f

... some future date, although I can't say the same about Oslo!
Yours faithfully
Bernard Wilson

g

Dear Sir,
I wish to make a complaint about a recent holiday to Copenhagen.
According to the brochure I received ...

1

h

... of the trip being seasick!
I would be grateful if you could make sure in ...

i

... with the Tivoli Gardens. What an experience! What an atmosphere!
And to think that it's in the centre ...

j

... Norway. However, what your brochure failed to mention was the fact
that the excursion was to be paid ...

k

... that time it was too late to go back! If I had realized how much it was
going to cost, I would certainly not have gone on it – especially since the
sea was so choppy that my wife and I spent most ...

First read all the segments to get a general idea of the two holidays, e.g.
one is to Spain, the other is to Copenhagen and Oslo. Then, see if you can
match beginnings and endings of segments. For example, *Apart* ... is
followed by ... *from*.

54 The perfect woman

This is a short story where all the lines are mixed up. We have given you the first line and the last line. Put the rest in the correct order.

My aunt Camilla died and left everything to ...

a .... once that she was the woman for him. He asked her for ....

b .... his taste. So he then went to Australia, but he couldn't find his perfect woman there either. Finally, Joe found himself back in his own country. Amazingly, within a few days of his return, he bumped ....

c .... into a lot of money too, and I have decided to go in search of the perfect man. I hope I find him.'

d .... her favourite nephew, Joe. Joe was unmarried, so he decided to use the money to go in search of ....   `1`

e .... on his cooking and the conversation flowed easily. Finally, as they sat drinking coffee, Joe told her all ....

f .... into a woman who was exactly what he was looking ....

g .... about Aunt Camilla's will and about his search for the perfect woman. 'That is amazing!' she exclaimed. 'I've just come ....

h .... for! Funnily enough, she lived near him, though he had never noticed her before. They met in the local supermarket. She dropped her purse. He picked it up and gave it to ....

i .... a date, and she accepted. After a few meetings, he finally invited her to have dinner with him. Everything ....

j .... the perfect woman. He went to America, but the women he met were just too loud or too quiet for ....

k .... went well during dinner. She complimented him ....

l .... her. She smiled and said thank you, and he knew at ....

Joe tried to smile, but it wasn't easy.

(Adapted from 'The Perfect Woman' in *Happy Days and Other Very Short Stories* by Jake Allsop, Penguin Books, 1998)

55 Idioms

Each sentence contains an idiom which uses a prepositional phrase.
Complete the sentences below with one of the following prepositions –
you will need to use some more than once.

at	by	from	in	into	on	out of	under	up to

1 She's very busy at the moment; she's _up to_ *her eyeballs in work*.

2 The police arrived just in time; they came _____ *the eleventh hour*.

3 He'll never pass the exam – *not* _____ *a month of Sundays*.

4 The goods were not sold openly but were available _____ *the counter*.

5 She never once needed to consult the instructions, she had all the information _____ *her fingertips*.

6 Since he has won Wimbledon, everyone wants to interview him. He's _____ *great demand*.

7 The boss didn't tell Kevin off for coming late. He must be _____ *her good books*.

8 He's almost dying; I'm afraid he's _____ *his last legs*.

9 There's nothing else she can do now – the matter is completely _____ *her hands*.

10 I know everything there is to know about Roman Britain. I know the subject _____ *A to Z*.

11 She rarely goes to the cinema – just *once* _____ *a blue moon*.

12 They had very little money but they survived. They lived _____ *a shoestring*.

13 He hasn't won yet – *not* _____ *a long shot*.

14 People arrived slowly, two or three at a time. They arrived _____ *dribs and drabs*.

15 Stop wasting time! Get to my office _____ *the double* !

16 I hate spiders. I *break* _____ *a cold sweat* just thinking about them.

Some idiomatic expressions, like, *not in a month of Sundays*, are easy to understand because they use common, everyday words. But often idioms use unusual words. For example, the words *dribs* and *drabs* only exist in the expression *in dribs and drabs*.

56 Cartoon time 2

Match the captions to the cartoons, adding the missing prepositions.

1 'Rubbish! There isn't a ship anywhere _____ sight!'

2 'Did you make that all _____ your own?'

3 'OK, so I'm hopeless _____ reading architects' drawings!'

4 'Actually, this is number 13. Number 14 is just _____ the corner.'

5 'Sorry, we don't start serving lunch _____ 12.30.'

6 'It's the only way I can stop the children getting _____ trouble.'

Section 8:
Just for fun!

This section contains some fun tests to help you revise prepositions in general.
Enjoy!

Girl: *My cousin's very good at bird impressions.*
Boy: *Really?*
Girl: *Yes. He eats worms!*

57 Confused consonants

Find the wrong letter in each of these newspaper headlines. What letter is needed so that the headline makes sense?

1

> HOME SECRETARY TO ƁOOK INTO PRISON CONDITIONS

L

2

> FIREMEN WARNED: 'DON'T PUMP TO CONCLUSIONS'

3

> MYSTERY EXPLOSION IN HOTEL: POLICE ARE BOOKING INTO IT

4

> CHICKEN BREEDER ON FRAUD CHARGE TOLD BY JUDGE: YOU WILL HAVE TO LAY FOR YOUR CRIMES

5

> HIGH-SPENDING LOCAL AUTHORITIES TOLD: 'MONEY DOESN'T GLOW ON TREES'

6

VETERINARY SURGEON ACCUSED OF CRUELTY TO CATS PROTESTS: 'PEOPLE LIKE TO PUSS OVER NOTHING'

7

GAMBLER CONVICTED OF MURDERING BOOKMAKER BETS FOR MERCY

8

FINANCIAL CRISIS IN SOCIAL DEMOCRAT PARTY: LEADER FALLS ON PARTY FAITHFUL TO COME TO THE RESCUE

9

WELFARE OFFICIALS ACCUSED OF CRYING INTO COUPLES' PRIVATE LIVES

10

WE CREAM ABOUT THE GOOD OLD DAYS, SAY PENSIONERS

58 What are they saying? 1

Supply the missing preposition(s) in each caption and then match it to the appropriate cartoon.

1 'What do you mean it's not that bad? I'm standing _____ my husband's shoulders!'

2 'What a pity you haven't brought your little dog _____ you. We were so looking forward _____ seeing him again.'

3 'Arthur's always been very sensitive _____ his bald spot.'

4 'I've decided _____ becoming a doctor – you have to wash your hands too often.'

5 'Is the banging _____ the wall keeping you awake, darling?'

6 'I'm tired _____ being Mr Nice Guy! I'm going to be much tougher _____ now on!'

59 Joke time 2

Complete the following jokes by filling in the missing prepositions.

1
Girl: My cousin's very good __at__ bird impressions.
Boy: Really?
Girl: Yes. He eats worms!

2
Walker: Tell me, will this path take me _____ the main road?
Local: No, Sir, you'll have to go _____ yourself.

3
Girl: You remind me _____ the sea.
Boy: Because I'm so wild and romantic?
Girl: No, because you make me sick!

4
Father: Johnny, I've had a letter _____ your headmaster. It seems you're very careless about your appearance.
Johnny: Am I, Dad?
Father: Yes, you haven't appeared _____ school at all this term.

5
BULLDOG _____ SALE:
Will eat anything. Very fond _____ children.

6
Woman 1: My husband's career is _____ ruins.
Woman 2: Oh, I am sorry to hear that.
Woman 1: There's nothing wrong _____ that. He's an archaeologist.

7
Piano tuner: I've come here to tune your piano.
Man: But we didn't send _____ you.
Piano tuner: No, but your neighbours did.

8
Mark: I understand that the sports and social club is looking _____ a treasurer.
Geoffrey: That's right.
Mark: But I thought the sports and social club only hired a treasurer a few months ago.
Geoffrey: They did. That's the treasurer they're looking _____!

9
I've always believed _____ love _____ first sight – ever since I looked _____ a mirror.

10
Teacher: What's the definition _____ 'minimum'?
Student: A very small mother.

60 What are they saying? 2

Supply the missing preposition(s) in each caption and then match it to the appropriate cartoon.

1 'I think we'd better apologise _____ them _____ waking them up.'

2 'It's amazing _____ me how people always seem to get married _____ alphabetical order.'

3 'This is the part I don't like – having to think _____ different names _____ them all.'

4 'Do I take it you object _____ my smoking a pipe?'

5 'Sorry – we don't have a menu. Just point _____ something _____ my apron.'

6 '_____ luck, we should be _____ London _____ nightfall.'

Answers

Test 1

1 opposite
2 on
3 under
4 above
5 to the left of / next to
6 next to / to the left of
7 in
8 between
9 behind
10 to the right of
11 below
12 in front of

Test 2

1 off
2 along/down/up
3 towards
4 On
5 after
6 on
7 across/through
8 along/up/down
9 through
10 at
11 along
12 to
13 over/across
14 In front of
15 to
16 At
17 in
18 in front of
19 round/around
20 to
21 of
22 under

Test 3

1 during	7 in
2 in	8 On
3 on	9 on
4 for	10 by
5 after	11 behind
6 in	12 on

13 within
14 after
15 at
16 from
17 to
18 past
19 by
20 until
21 in
22 since
23 for
24 on
25 in

Test 4

1 in future
2 out of date
3 at times
4 at the moment
5 From time to time
6 not for long
7 in the end
8 without delay
9 in progress
10 In the meantime
11 in season
12 in no time
13 to this day
14 for the time being
15 before long

Test 5

1 over, above
2 in, at
3 on, on to
4 below, under
5 into, in
6 to, at
7 before, in front of
8 on, in
9 in, at
10 At, In
11 since, for
12 between, among
13 out of, outside
14 over, above
15 until, at
16 within, by
17 through, during
18 next to, near
19 by, on
20 under, below

Test 6

1	from	7	After
2	to, into/through	8	into
3	in/for	9	from, on
4	in	10	on, at, for
5	in/during, at	11	into
6	on		

Section 2: Verb + preposition

Test 7

1	e	7	h
2	a	8	i
3	l	9	f
4	j	10	c
5	d	11	g
6	k	12	b

Test 8

1 hear about
2 arrived at
3 belongs to
4 apologize for
5 fill in
6 vote against
7 distinguish between
8 complained to
9 corresponds to
10 knocking at
11 rhymes with
12 experiment on
13 pray for/with
14 suffered from
15 losing at
16 died from

Test 9

AT: glance, hint, marvel, point, wink
FOR: apply, cater, compensate, long, vote
FROM: abstain, benefit, depart, expel, flee
IN: believe, decrease, delight, indulge, invest
OF: approve, consist, dispose, dream, take advantage
ON: concentrate, depend, enrol, rely, tread
TO: appeal, dedicate, object, respond, subscribe
WITH: coincide, collaborate, cope, quarrel, sympathize

Test 10

1 translated into
2 book into
3 tastes of
4 accused of
5 deal with
6 grumble about
7 surrounded by
8 insists/insisted on
9 specializes in
10 count on
11 account for
12 refrain from

Test 11

1 raving about
2 looking after
3 agree with
4 taken to
5 elaborate on
6 jumped at
7 count against
8 get round
9 eaten into
10 plough through
11 stumbled across
12 put towards
13 stick by
14 indulge in
15 gloss over
16 vouch for

Test 12

1	over	8	at
2	in	9	against
3	against	10	over/through
4	in	11	against
5	for	12	at
6	at	13	for
7	by	14	by

Test 13

1	about	8	on
2	on	9	from
3	into	10	on
4	from	11	into
5	about	12	about
6	to	13	to
7	on		

Test 14

1 roared with
2 care for
3 stand for
4 sheltered from
5 borrowed ... from
6 called for
7 collided with
8 come into
9 named after (British English)/
  named for (American English)
10 go after/go for
11 appeals to
12 fell for
13 prevent ... (from)
14 driving at

Test 15

1 out for	9 up with
2 over to	10 up on
3 behind with	11 in with
4 around for	12 down to
5 in for	13 up to
6 down with	14 on at
7 away with	15 back on
8 around to	16 away for

Test 16

Across

2 prefers
5 hide
7 travelled
10 shouting
11 among
13 near
15 into
17 join
18 between
20 against
21 from
24 multiply
26 from
27 note
28 with

Down

1 shelter
3 for
4 exchange
6 down
8 about
9 escape
12 go
14 longs
15 invited
16 of
19 worry
22 blame
23 mixing
25 left
26 flow
29 to

Section 3: Noun + preposition

Test 17

1 g	5 j	9 a
2 e	6 i	10 l
3 k	7 h	11 d
4 c	8 b	12 f

Test 18

1 opposite of
2 problem with
3 choice between
4 excuse for
5 knowledge of
6 objection to
7 fall in
8 freedom from
9 genius at
10 basis for
11 control over
12 Cruelty to
13 strain on
14 campaign against
15 anger against

Test 19

1 at a cost of
2 at peace with
3 by means of
4 for the benefit of
5 in agreement with
6 in answer to
7 on behalf of
8 on good terms with
9 out of pity for
10 under the influence of
11 with reference to
12 with the compliments of

Test 20

1 on		9 for
2 to		10 into, into
3 with		11 from
4 in		12 of
5 on		13 to
6 in		14 into
7 in		15 to
8 for		

Test 21

1 a relative of
2 notice of
3 reduction in
4 pleasure in
5 impression with/impression on
6 confidence in
7 talent for
8 impact on
9 exceptions to
10 demand for
11 connection between
12 expert in/on

Test 22

1	for	9	about
2	in	10	in
3	at	11	by
4	for	12	over
5	of	13	in
6	on/about	14	for
7	with	15	to
8	of		

Test 23

1 in exchange for
2 in common with
3 in addition to
4 in favour of
5 at odds with
6 at the expense of
7 with respect to
8 with the exception of
9 for the sake of
10 out of regard for
11 on account of
12 by virtue of

Test 24

Across		Down	
4	increase	1	Cruelty
6	of	2	between
8	reputation	3	towards
11	leave	5	cheque
13	difficulty	7	in
14	over	9	off
16	with	10	solution
18	Hold	12	from
20	against	15	engagement
21	recipe	17	advice
24	Tell	19	over
25	quotation	22	for
		23	ran
		24	to

Section 4: Preposition + noun (1)

Test 25

AT: first, dawn, least, lunch
BY: accident, heart, name, Salvador
Dali
IN: a moment, fact, future, private
ON: holiday, sale, schedule, strike

Test 26

1	sight	9	own
2	account	10	behaviour
3	time	11	approval
4	market	12	impulse
5	hold	13	credit
6	order	14	business
7	journey	15	holiday
8	diet		

Test 27

1	(d) hospital	9	(b) luxury
2	(l) pain	10	(m) disguise
3	(i) detail	11	(e) focus
4	(g) public	12	(j) doubt
5	(o) love	13	(a) fashion
6	(c) existence	14	(f) general
7	(k) difficulty	15	(h) fact
8	(n) future		

Test 28

1	in	8	at
2	in	9	in
3	by	10	on
4	out of	11	out of
5	on	12	at
6	at	13	out of
7	by	14	at

Test 29

1	at	9	at
2	on	10	under
3	at	11	on
4	against	12	under
5	on	13	off
6	against	14	off
7	off	15	Under
8	under		

Test 30

1	n	8	g
2	k	9	b
3	j	10	l
4	h	11	d
5	a	12	e
6	i	13	f
7	m	14	c

Test 31

1	b)	10	a)
2	c)	11	b)
3	a)	12	a)
4	c)	13	b)
5	b)	14	c)
6	b)	15	b)
7	a)	16	a)
8	c)	17	b)
9	c)		

Test 32

A
1 in, in
2 against
3 Between
4 up
5 in
6 in
7 over
8 from
9 with
10 out of
11 Out of, out of
12 Out of, into
13 before
14 on
15 without

B	a	9	i	8
	b	3	j	2
	c	15	k	12
	d	6	l	14
	e	1	m	11
	f	10	n	5
	g	13	o	7
	h	4		

Section 5: Preposition + noun (2)

Test 33

1 (o) full speed
2 (l) a guess
3 (h) a distance
4 (n) dawn
5 (m) first
6 (k) home
7 (c) a disadvantage
8 (a) a discount
9 (e) least
10 (g) night
11 (f) war
12 (i) short notice
13 (j) the moment
14 (b) your own risk
15 (d) first hand

Test 34

1	boat	8	means
2	way	9	profession
3	air	10	nature
4	cheque	11	surprise
5	law	12	marriage
6	ear	13	force
7	appointment	14	accident

Test 35

1 in favour of
2 at the end
3 by name
4 in front of
5 In view of
6 by sight
7 in time
8 In case of
9 at heart
10 in time of
11 divide it among
12 in principle
13 for fear of
14 in the possession of

Test 36

1	b	9	h
2	d	10	f
3	o	11	j
4	c	12	i
5	m	13	a
6	g	14	e
7	l	15	k
8	n		

Test 37

1 garden
2 bed
3 hurry
4 debt
5 condition
6 advance
7 case
8 danger
9 mood
10 emergency
11 taste
12 code
13 confidence
14 conclusion
15 moderation

Test 38

1 from memory
2 on good terms
3 in secret
4 age of
5 outskirts of
6 mood for
7 by herself
8 habit of
9 out of stock
10 under pressure
11 in self-defence
12 with any luck
13 for good
14 by mistake

Test 39

1	in	8	in
2	for	9	at
3	After	10	after
4	for	11	for
5	to	12	for
6	at	13	After
7	after/at	14	at

Test 40

1 on, in (picture b)
2 at (picture f)
3 in (picture e)
4 On (picture a)
5 at (picture c)
6 on (picture d)

Section 6: Adjective + preposition

Test 41

AT: hopeless, quick, surprised, valued
OF: aware, jealous, regardless, short
FOR: famous, handy, late, ready
TO: according, accustomed, opposed, similar
WITH: annoyed, friendly, pleased, popular

Test 42

1 interested in
2 famous for
3 doubtful about
4 valued at
5 valid for
6 handy for
7 similar to

8 incapable of
9 crazy about
10 grateful to
11 popular with
12 characteristic of
13 typical of
14 new to

Test 43

1 sympathetic to
2 quick with/quick at
3 envious of
4 unaware of
5 sensitive to
6 deep in
7 suited to
8 exempt from
9 fortunate in
10 distracted by
11 allergic to

Test 44

1	at	7	with/at
2	at/by	8	in
3	about/by	9	of
4	in	10	for
5	with	11	on
6	on	12	of

Test 45

1 contrary to
2 missing from
3 disgusted at/by
4 familiar with
5 short of
6 different from/to
7 identical to
8 peculiar to
9 subject to
10 well known for
11 mad about/on
12 According to
13 due to
14 delighted by/with

Test 46

1 bad at
2 jealous of
3 addicted to
4 surprised at
5 famous for
6 based on
7 followed by
8 angry with/at
9 involved in
10 full of
11 expert at
12 disqualified from
13 capable of

Test 47

1 c (accustomed)
2 j (late)
3 m (due)
4 e (pleased)
5 i (keen)
6 g (nervous)
7 n (hopeless)
8 l (opposed)
9 d (regardless)
10 a (convenient)
11 b (suspicious)
12 h (accompanied)
13 k (rich)
14 f (blind)

Test 48

Across	Down
2 about	1 absent
3 married	5 covered
4 accustomed	6 engrossed
8 sorry	7 typical
9 afraid	10 descended
11 good	11 grateful
12 successful	13 fluent
14 satisfied	15 tired
18 suitable	16 famous
19 with	17 guilty

Section 7: Prepositions in context

Test 49

1 On/During		13 on
2 in/to		14 through
3 for		15 into
4 in/during		16 By
5 in		17 for
6 for		18 in
7 through		19 next
8 to		20 for
9 in		21 to
10 into		22 to
11 of		23 from/off
12 with		

Test 50

A	a 9	d 3	g 8
	b 4	e 1	h 6
	c 7	f 5	i 2

Dear Bob,
Sorry I've taken such a long time in answering your letter. The truth is that I've been really busy these past few weeks … with exams and everything. I hope you understand.

My main reason for writing is to ask if you'd like to spend a couple of weeks with us … in the summer. Mum and Dad have rented a caravan in Fairlight – a little village … near Hastings. They thought you might like to join us for two weeks – from 2–15 August. It sleeps four, so there's plenty of room. And it's only five minutes … from the sea, so we could go swimming every day. It should be great fun, but it would be even better if you could be there too. So what do you say? Apart … from this, there's not much to say really. Dad's got a new car – a Volvo – and Mum's just started back to work again.

By the way, Dad asked me to find … out if your parents received the holiday brochures he sent, as he hasn't heard … from them yet.

Well, Bob, that's all for now. I hope you're keeping well and that you'll be able to join us … in the summer.

Give my regards to your parents and write soon.
Lots of love
Paul

B a 10   e 6   i 7
   b 3   f 8   j 4
   c 2   g 1
   d 9   h 5

Dear Paul

Many thanks for your letter. It was good to hear from you at last (I was beginning to think you had emigrated or something!).

About the summer, yes, of ... course I'd love to join you and your parents in Fairlight. It sounds really fun. I visited Hastings once and it was a really nice place – lots ... of things to do – especially in the summer. So thank your parents for me and tell them I'm really looking forward to it. I asked Mum and Dad ... about the holiday brochures. They haven't received them yet (you know what the post is like!). But they'll write as soon as they get them, and they asked me to tell you to thank your Dad ... for all the trouble he's gone to.

By the way, Paul, Dad's very jealous ... of the new Volvo. He's always liked foreign cars – especially Volvos – and keeps hinting ... to Mum about getting a new car. But she's not interested really, so I don't think he'll persuade her.

Well, Paul, I'll stop now because I'm off to a disco ... with Sally. You remember Sally, don't you? She was the girl I met at Jenny's birthday party. We've been together now ... for almost three months (not bad for me!). What about you? Are you still going out with Pauline or have you got someone new now?

Anyway, do write some time and remember to give my love ... to your Mum and Dad.

Lots of love
Bob

Test 51

1 (k) beyond a joke
2 (o) under water
3 (h) at present
4 (f) for ever
5 (j) on paper
6 (c) with care
7 (b) in blossom
8 (n) for breakfast
9 (d) on my knees
10 (g) out of the question
11 (m) on the job
12 (a) out of the blue
13 (l) under arrest
14 (i) after dark
15 (e) in gear

Test 52

1 in		14 to
2 At		15 In
3 after		16 to
4 in		17 to
5 to		18 to
6 about		19 on
7 to		20 to
8 for		21 from
9 with		22 by
10 with		23 of
11 of		24 at
12 from		25 in
13 in		

Test 53

A a 12   f 13   k 10
   b 11   g 7   l 2
   c 5   h 9   m 8
   d 1   i 3
   e 4   j 6

Dear Sir,

I have just returned from a holiday in Spain and all I can say is that it was a nightmare from ... start to finish! When I chose Sunthorn Holidays, I was under the impression that I was dealing ... with a company I could rely on. How wrong could I have been?

The trouble started even before ... our departure. To begin with, the plane was overbooked. This meant that myself and ten other passengers were forced to go on another plane – one hour later! Unfortunately, our luggage was still ... on the first plane so that there was a further delay in ... sorting out the mess when we finally arrived at the airport in Spain.

The 'luxury' hotel as advertised in your holiday brochure was still under ... construction, which meant that there was the constant sound of cement mixers – hardly the peaceful and relaxing holiday I had been looking forward to.

My room was much smaller than I had expected and throughout ... my stay, I never once managed to get the shower to work properly – the water was either too hot or too cold.

Another thing: in your brochure you state that the hotel is only a few minutes from ... the sea. Twenty-five to be exact! And what a beach! It was so polluted that it was positively dangerous ... to one's health.

Finally, on the return journey, I was made to sit ... in an aisle seat despite the fact that I had specifically asked ... for a seat next to the window.

This is the worst holiday I have ever had in my life, and I demand my money back. If not, I shall put the matter in the hands of my solicitor.

I look forward ... to hearing from you soon.

Yours faithfully
Pauline Wood

B a 7   e 2   i 9
  b 4   f 11   j 3
  c 8   g 1   k 5
  d 10   h 6

Dear Sir,
I wish to make a complaint about a recent holiday to Copenhagen.
According to the brochure I received ... from Sunthorn Holidays, the holiday was to include a two-day boat trip to Olso in ... Norway. However, what your brochure failed to mention was the fact that the excursion was to be paid ... for separately! Unfortunately, our travel representative forgot to mention this fact until we were well at sea! By ... that time it was too late to go back! If I had realised how much it was going to cost, I would certainly not have gone on it – especially since the sea was so choppy that my wife and I spent most ... of the trip being seasick!
    I would be grateful if you could make sure in ... future that all 'extra' costs are clearly shown in your brochure.
    Apart ... from the above, the rest of our holiday in Copenhagen was wonderful, and both my wife and I fell in love ... with the Tivoli Gardens. What an experience! What an atmosphere! And to think that it's in the centre ... of the city. Whatever happens, we shall certainly return to Copenhagen at ... some future date, although I can't say the same about Oslo!
Yours faithfully
Bernard Wilson

Test 54

a 7   g 11
b 3   h 5
c 12   i 8
d 1   j 2
e 10   k 9
f 4   l 6

My aunt Camilla died and left everything to ... her favourite nephew, Joe. Joe was unmarried, so he decided to use the money to go in search of ... the perfect woman. He went to America, but the women he met were just too loud or too quiet for ... his taste. So he then went to Australia, but he couldn't find his perfect woman there either. Finally, Joe found ... himself back in his own country. Amazingly, within a few days of his return, he bumped ... into a woman who was exactly what he was looking ... for! Funnily enough, she lived near him, though he had never noticed her before. They met in the local supermarket. She dropped her purse. He picked it up and gave it to ... her. She smiled and said thank you, and he knew at ... once that she was the woman for him. He asked her for ... a date, and she accepted. After a few meetings, he finally invited her to have dinner with him. Everything ... went well during dinner. She complimented him ... on his cooking and the conversation flowed easily. Finally, as they sat drinking coffee, Joe told her all ... about Aunt Camilla's will and about his search for the perfect woman. 'That is amazing!' she exclaimed. 'I've just come ... into a lot of money too, and I have decided to go in search of the perfect man. I hope I find him.' ... Joe tried to smile, but it wasn't easy.

Test 55

1	up to	9	out of
2	at	10	from
3	in	11	in
4	under	12	on
5	at	13	by
6	in	14	in
7	in	15	at
8	on	16	into

Test 56

1 in (picture e)
2 on (picture a)
3 at (picture d)
4 round (picture c)
5 until (picture b)
6 into (picture f)

Section 8: Just for fun!

Test 57

1 HOME SECRETARY TO **LOOK** INTO PRISON CONDITIONS
2 FIREMEN WARNED: 'DON'T **JUMP** TO CONCLUSIONS'
3 MYSTERY EXPLOSION IN HOTEL: POLICE ARE **LOOKING** INTO IT

4 CHICKEN BREEDER ON FRAUD CHARGE TOLD BY JUDGE: YOU WILL HAVE TO **PAY** FOR YOUR CRIMES
5 HIGH-SPENDING LOCAL AUTHORITIES TOLD: 'MONEY DOESN'T **GROW** ON TREES'
6 VETERINARY SURGEON ACCUSED OF CRUELTY TO CATS PROTESTS: 'PEOPLE LIKE TO **FUSS** OVER NOTHING'
7 GAMBLER CONVICTED OF MURDERING BOOKMAKER **BEGS** FOR MERCY
8 FINANCIAL CRISIS IN SOCIAL DEMOCRAT PARTY: LEADER **CALLS** ON PARTY FAITHFUL TO COME TO THE RESCUE
9 WELFARE OFFICIALS ACCUSED OF **PRYING** INTO COUPLES' PRIVATE LIVES
10 WE **DREAM** ABOUT THE GOOD OLD DAYS, SAY PENSIONERS

Test 58
1 on (picture d)
2 with, to (picture c)
3 about (picture f)
4 against (picture b)
5 on (picture a)
6 of, from (picture e)

Test 59
1 at
2 to, by
3 of
4 from, at/in
5 for, of
6 in, with
7 for
8 for, for
9 in, at, in
10 of

Test 60
1 to, for (picture b)
2 to, in (picture d)
3 of/up, for (picture f)
4 to (picture e)
5 to, on (picture a)
6 With, in, by (picture c)

Test Your way to success in English
Test Your Vocabulary

0582 45166 3

0582 45167 1

0582 45168 X

0582 45169 8

0582 45170 1

Test Your way to success in English

Test Your Professional English

Test Your way to success in English
Test Your Grammar and Skills

0582 45176 0

0582 45171 X

0582 45172 8

0582 45173 6

0582 45175 2

0582 45174 4

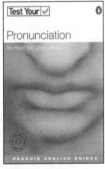

0582 46902 3

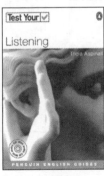

0582 46908 2

0582 46905 8